# WHAT NONSENSE!
## &
# ILLUMINATED LIMERICKS

**Roger Kilroy**

**Illustrations by
Ann Axworthy
McLachlan**

CHANCELLOR
PRESS

*What Nonsense!* first published in 1978 by Knight Books
*Illuminated Limericks* first published in 1982 by Corgi

This collected volume first published in 1995 by Chancellor Press
an imprint of Reed Consumer Books Limited
Michelin House, 81 Fulham Road, London SW3 6RB
and Auckland, Singapore, Melbourne and Toronto

ISBN: 1 85152 695 1

A CIP catalogue record for this book is available from the British Library

Printed in Great Britain by Cox & Wyman Limited

# WHAT NONSENSE!
## &
# ILLUMINATED LIMERICKS

# WHAT NONSENSE!

# *Contents*

# *Introduction*

Once upon a time – well, to be exact, it was the afternoon of 14th December 1970 – I was visiting one of the world's great Art Galleries. It was the Louvre Museum in Paris, where you'll find, among other perfect pictures and sculptures and works of art, the world's most famous painting: the Mona Lisa by Leonardo da Vinci. It is an extraordinary painting, a very special painting, a painting you must go and see for yourself if ever you get the chance, but as it happens, on that particular December afternoon, it wasn't the Mona Lisa that caught my eye. It was the painting right next door to it.

This painting was of a bowl of fruit and underneath it was a little notice that read: 'Catal 1673'. Now, I don't know much about art and I'd never heard of this painter called Catal, but I certainly liked the bowl of fruit he painted in 1673. Having admired it, I moved on to another room in the museum where I was pleased and surprised to find another painting I liked very much. This one was of a man playing a mandolin and the notice underneath it said: 'Catal 1760'. Well, I thought to myself, this character Catal lived to a ripe old age if he was painting bowls of fruit back in 1673 and was still hard at it painting men and mandolins in 1760. But it wasn't until I got into the next room that my eyes almost popped out of my head. There was an enormous painting of the River Thames, with written underneath it: 'Catal 1829'! Now what on earth was the explanation of this? Did Catal live for two hundred years? Was this Catal the son of the other Catal? Or the grandson? Or the great nephew? Or the second cousin twice removed? Or what?

9

Well, the answer, as you've probably guessed, is that Catal wasn't a painter at all. On the notices underneath the pictures in the Louvre Museum the word 'Catal' is simply short for 'Catalogue Number'! So the bowl of fruit was item 1,673 in the catalogue and the man playing the mandolin was item 1,760 and the painting of the River Thames was item 1,829. It was all as simple – and as silly – as that.

I've told you this story in case you happen to be someone who has just read through the Contents list of this book and thought to yourself, 'My goodness, this fellow Anon has written an awful lot of comic verse!'

Anon, of course, is no more a person who writes poetry than Catal is a person who paints. Anon is short for Anonymous. And the reason you'll find Anon cropping up so often in the pages that follow is that there are so very many delightfully dotty poems whose authors are unknown. I can't give you the name of the writer who invented the Limerick, but even if you wouldn't know what to call him if you met him in the street – and, frankly, you are unlikely to meet him since the first Limerick appeared in 1822 – I don't see why you shouldn't enjoy his witty verses all the same.

Most of the shorter poems in this collection are by unknown authors. Most of the longer ones aren't. Probably the best-known of all the famous writers of comic verse are Edward Lear (1812–1888), who wrote five fantastic books of nonsense, Lewis Carroll (1832–1898), who created Alice in Wonderland and so much else besides, and William Schwenck Gilbert (1836–1911), who wrote the words for all those glorious Gilbert and Sullivan comic operas. Naturally enough, all three of these giants are generously represented in the book.

As well as Lear, Carroll and Gilbert, all three of whom

are best known for their humorous verses, you will also find here poems by writers who are best known for work that is much more serious. Samuel Taylor Coleridge (1772–1834), Henry Wadsworth Longfellow (1807–1882), Oliver Wedell Holmes (1809–1894), Christina Rossetti (1830–1894) and Thomas Hood (1835–1874) are all very famous poets, but not many people realise that they wrote light-hearted verses as well as their more solemn master-pieces. In the same way, you may have heard of William Thackeray (1811–1863), who wrote a great novel called *Vanity Fair*, and Robert Louis Stevenson (1850–1894), who wrote *Treasure Island*, but you probably didn't know that both important writers also wrote comic gems.

As far as I'm concerned, whether the authors of the verses in this book are terribly famous or totally unknown (or, in fact, like most of them, somewhere in between), doesn't matter a bit. What matters to me are the verses themselves. And the only reason for choosing the ones that are here is that they are my favourites. Of all the thousands of poems that I've read, the hundred or more that I've chosen for this book are the ones that made me smile most broadly and chuckle loudest. Some of them are what you'd call 'funny peculiar'. Some of them are 'funny ha-ha'. To me, all of them are a delight. And I hope that you'll enjoy reading them as much as I've enjoyed collecting them.

GYLES BRANDRETH

# What Nonsense!

Anon

One fine October morning
  In September, last July,
The moon lay thick upon the ground,
  The snow shone in the sky;
The flowers were singing gaily
  And the birds were in full bloom,
I went down to the cellar
  To sweep the upstair room.

# The Broom, the Shovel, the Poker and the Tongs

## Edward Lear

The Broom and the Shovel, the Poker and Tongs,
    They all took a drive in the Park,
And they each sang a song, Ding-a-dong, Ding-a-dong,
    Before they each went back in the dark.
Mr Poker he sat quite upright in the coach,
    Mr Tongs made a clatter and clash,
Miss Shovel was dressed all in black (with a brooch),
    Mrs Broom was in blue (with a sash).
        Ding-a-dong! Ding-a-dong!
        And they all sang a song!

'O Shovely so lovely!' the Poker he sang,
    'You have perfectly conquered my heart!
'Ding-a-dong! Ding-a-dong! If you're pleased with my
        song,
    'I will feed you with cold apple tart!
'When you scrape on the coals with a delicate sound,
    'You enrapture my life with delight!
'Your nose is so shiny! Your head is so round!
    'And your shape is so slender and bright!
        'Ding-a-dong! Ding-a-dong!
        'Ain't you pleased with my song?'

'Alas! Mrs Broom!' sighed the Tongs in his song,
    'O is it because I'm so thin,
'And my legs are so long – Ding-a-dong! Ding-a-dong!
    'That you don't care about me a pin?

14

'Ah, fairest of creatures, when sweeping the room,
    'Ah! why don't you heed my complaint!
'Must you needs be so cruel, you beautiful Broom,
    'Because you are covered with paint?
        'Ding-a-dong! Ding-a-dong!'
        And they all sang a song

Mrs Broom and Miss Shovel together they sang,
    'What nonsense you're singing today!'
Said the Shovel, 'I'll certainly hit you a bang!'
    Said the Broom, 'And I'll sweep you away!'
So the Coachman drove homeward as fast as he could,
    Perceiving their anger with pain;
But they put on the kettle, and little by little,
    They all became happy again.
        Ding-a-dong!
        There's an end of my song!

## The First Limerick

### Anon

There was a sick man of Tobago
Lived long on rice-gruel and sago;
    But at last, to his bliss,
    The physician said this:
'To a roast leg of mutton you may go.'

# Montezuma's Pie

## D. F. Alderson

Montezuma
  Met a puma
Coming through the rye;
  Montezuma
  Made the puma
Into apple-pie.

  Invitation
  To the nation
Everyone to come.
  Montezuma
  And the puma
Give a kettle-drum.

  Acceptation
  Of the nation,
One and all invited.
  Montezuma
  And the puma
Equally delighted.

  Preparation,
  Ostentation,
Dresses rich prepared:
  Feathers – jewels –
  Work in crewels –
No expense is spared.

Congregation
Of the nation
Round the palace wall.
Awful rumour
That the puma
Won't be served at all.

Deputation
From the nation,
Audience they gain.
'What's this rumour?
Montezuma,
If you please, explain.'

Montezuma
(Playful humour
Very well sustained)
Answers 'Pie-dish,
And it's my dish,
Is for me retained.'

Exclamation!
Indignation!
Feeling running high.
Montezuma
Joins the puma
In the apple-pie.

# *Epicurious*

## Anon

An epicure, dining at Crewe,
Found quite a large mouse in his stew;
    Said the waiter: 'Don't shout
    And wave it about,
Or the rest will be wanting one, too!'

# Topsy-Turvey World

## William Brighty Rands

If the butterfly courted the bee,
  And the owl the porcupine;
If churches were built in the sea,
  And three times one were nine;
If the pony rode his master,
  If the buttercups ate the cows,
If the cat had the dire disaster
  To be worried, sir, by the mouse;
If mamma, sir, sold the baby
  To a gipsy for half a crown;
If a gentleman, sir, was a lady, –
  The world would be Upside-Down!
If any or all of these wonders
Should ever come about,
I should not consider them blunders,
  For I should be Inside-Out!

# Mr Nobody

## Anon

I know a funny little man,
    As quiet as a mouse.
He does the mischief that is done
    In everybody's house.
Though no one ever sees his face,
    Yet one and all agree
That every plate we break, was cracked
    By Mr Nobody.


'Tis he who always tears our books,
    Who leaves the door ajar.
He picks the buttons from our shirts,
    And scatters pins afar.
That squeaking door will always squeak
    For prithee, don't you see?
We leave the oiling to be done
    By Mr Nobody.


He puts the damp wood upon the fire,
    That kettles will not boil:
His are the feet that bring in mud
    And all the carpets soil.
The papers that so oft are lost –
    Who had them last but he?
There's no one tosses them about
    But Mr Nobody.

The fingermarks upon the door
  By none of us were made.
We never leave the blinds unclosed
  To let the curtains fade.
The ink we never spill! The boots
  That lying round you see,
Are not our boots – they all belong
  To Mr Nobody.


# Whistling Girls

## Anon

Grandma said, 'It's a very queer thing;
Boys must whistle and girls must sing.
That's how it is,' I heard her say.
'The same tomorrow as yesterday.'

Grandma said when I asked her why
Girls couldn't whistle the same as I,
'Son, you know it's a natural thing
For boys to whistle and for girls to sing.'

Grandma said, ' 'Twould never do;
An' there's a very good reason, too:
Whistling girls an' crowing hens
Always come to some bad ends.'

# Fidgety Phil

## Heinrich Hoffman

Let me see if Philip can
Be a little gentleman:
Let me see if he is able
To sit still for once at table:
Thus Papa bade Phil behave;
And Mama look'd very grave.
But fidgety Phil,
He won't sit still;
He wriggles
And giggles,
And then, I declare,
Swings backwards and forwards
And tilts up his chair,
Just like any rocking-horse; —
'Philip! I am getting cross!'

See the naughty restless child
Growing still more rude and wild,
Till his chair falls over quite.
Philip screams with all his might,
Catches at the cloth, but then
That makes matters worse again.
Down upon the ground they fall,
Glasses, plates, knives, forks and all.

How Mama did fret and frown,
When she saw them tumbling down!
And Papa made such a face!
Philip is in sad disgrace.

Where is Philip, where is he?
Fairly cover'd up, you see!
Cloth and all are lying on him:
He has pull'd down all upon him.
What a terrible to-do!
Dishes, glasses, snapt in two!
Here a knife, and there a fork!
Philip, this is cruel work.

Table all so bare, and ah!
Poor Papa and poor Mamma
Look quite cross, and wonder how
They shall make their dinner now.

# The Young Man of Japan

## Anon

There was a young man of Japan
Whose limericks never would scan;
   When they said it was so,
   He replied, 'Yes, I know,
But I always try to get as many words into the last line as
         ever I possibly can.'

# The Young Lady of Riga

Anon

There was a young lady of Riga
Who went for a ride on a tiger:
    They returned from the ride
    With the lady inside
And a smile on the face of the tiger.

# The Young Lady of Spain

Anon

There was a young lady of Spain
Who was dreadfully sick in a train,
   Not once, but again,
   And again and again,
And again and again and again.


# The Old Person of Fratton

Anon

There was an old person of Fratton
Who would go to church with his hat on.
   'If I wake up,' he said,
   'With my hat on my head,
I shall know that it hasn't been sat on.'

# The Ruler of the Queen's Navee

## W. S. Gilbert

When I was a lad I served a term
As office boy to an Attorney's firm.
I cleaned the windows and I swept the floor,
And I polished up the handle of the big front door.
  I polished up that handle so carefulee
  That now I am the Ruler of the Queen's Navee!

As office boy I made such a mark
That they gave me the post of a junior clerk.
I served the writs with a smile so bland,
And I copied all the letters in a big round hand –
  I copied all the letters in a hand so free,
  That now I am the Ruler of the Queen's Navee!

In serving writs I made such a name
That an articled clerk I soon became;
I wore clean collars and a brand-new suit
For the pass examination at the Institute.
  And that pass examination did so well for me,
  That now I am the Ruler of the Queen's Navee!

Of legal knowledge I acquired such a grip
That they took me into the partnership.
And that junior partnership, I ween,
Was the only ship that I ever had seen.
  But that kind of ship so suited me,
  That now I am the Ruler of the Queen's Navee!

I grew so rich that I was sent
By a pocket borough into Parliament.
I always voted at my party's call,
And I never thought of thinking for myself at all.
    I thought so little, they rewarded me
    By making me the Ruler of the Queen's Navee!

Now landsmen all, whoever you may be,
If you want to rise to the top of the tree,
If your soul isn't fettered to an office stool,
Be careful to be guided by this golden rule –
    Stick close to your desks and never go to sea,
    And you all may be Rulers of the Queen's Navee!

## *My Epitaph*

### Anon

Here lie I, bereft of breath,
Because a cough
Carried me off;
Then a coffin
They carried me off in.

# Animals I have Known

## Nixon Waterman

A thick-fleeced lamb came trotting by:
'Pray whither now, my lamb,' quoth I.
'To have,' said he with ne'er a stop,
'My wool clipped at the baa-baa shop.'

I asked the dog: 'Why all this din?'
Said he: 'I'm fashioned outside in,
And all my days and nights I've tried
My best to get the bark outside.'

A hen was cackling loud and long,
Said I to her: 'How strange your song!'
Said she: ' 'Tis scarce a song; in fact
It is a lay, to be eggs-act.'

I asked the cat: 'Pray tell me why
You love to sing?' She blinked her eye.
'My purr-puss, sir, as you can see,
Is to a-mews myself,' said she.

A horse was being lashed one day.
Said I: 'Why don't you run away?'
'Neigh, neigh! my stable mind,' said he,
'Still keeps its equine-imity.'

I asked the cow: 'Why don't you kick
The man who whips you with the stick?'
'Alas, I must be lashed,' said she,
'That I may give whipped cream, you see!'

# *Obvious Reasons*

## Lewis Carroll

There was once a young man of Oporta
Who daily got shorter and shorter,
  The reason he said
  Was the hod on his head,
Which was filled with the heaviest mortar.

His sister named Lucy O'Finner,
Grew constantly thinner and thinner,
  The reason was plain,
  She slept out in the rain,
And was never allowed any dinner.

# The Animal Alphabet

## Anon

Alligator, beetle, porcupine, whale,
Bobolink, panther, dragon-fly, snail,
Dromedary, leopard, mud-turtle, bear,
Elephant, badger, pelican, ox,
Flying-fish, reindeer, anaconda, fox,
Guinea-pig, dolphin, antelope, goose,
Humming-bird, weasel, pickerel, moose,
Ibex, rhinoceros, owl, kangaroo,
Jackal, opossum, toad, cockatoo,
Kingfisher, peacock, anteater, bat,
Lizard, ichneumon, honey-bee, rat,
Mocking-bird, camel, grasshopper, mouse,
Nightingale, spider, cuttle-fish, grouse,
Ocelot, pheasant, wolverine, auk,
Periwinkle, ermine, katydid, hawk,
Quail, hippopotamus, armadillo, moth,
Rattlesnake, lion, woodpecker, sloth,
Salamander, goldfinch, angleworm, dog,
Tiger, flamingo, scorpion, frog,
Unicorn, ostrich, nautilus, mole,
Viper, gorilla, basilisk, sole,
Whippoorwill, beaver, centipede, fawn,
Xantho, canary, polliwog, swan,
Yellowhammer, eagle, hyena, lark,
Zebra, chameleon, butterfly, shark.

# *The Mad Gardener's Song*

## Lewis Carroll

He thought he saw an Elephant,
    That practised on a fife:
He looked again, and found it was
    A Letter from his Wife.
'At length I realise,' he said,
    'The bitterness of Life!'

He thought he saw a Buffalo
    Upon the chimney-piece:
He looked again, and found it was
    His Sister's Husband's Niece.
'Unless you leave this house,' he said,
    'I'll send for the Police!'

He thought he saw a Rattlesnake
    That questioned him in Greek:
He looked again, and found it was
    The Middle of Next Week.
'The one thing I regret,' he said,
    'Is that it cannot speak!'

He thought he saw a Banker's Clerk
    Descending from the 'bus:
He looked again, and found it was
    A Hippopotamus.
'If this should stay to dine,' he said,
    'There won't be much for us!'

He thought he saw a Kangaroo
   That worked a coffee-mill:
He looked again, and found it was
   A Vegetable-Pill.
'Were I to swallow this,' he said,
   'I should be very ill!'

He thought he saw a Coach-and-Four
   That stood beside his bed:
He looked again, and found it was
   A Bear without a Head.
'Poor thing,' he said, 'poor silly thing!
   It's waiting to be fed!'

He thought he saw an Albatross
   That fluttered round the lamp:
He looked again, and found it was
   A Penny-Postage-Stamp.
'You'd best be getting home,' he said,
   'The nights are very damp!'

He thought he saw a Garden-Door
   That opened with a key:
He looked again, and found it was
   A Double Rule of Three:
'And all its mystery,' he said,
   'Is clear as day to me!'

He thought he saw an Argument
   That proved he was the Pope:
He looked again, and found it was
   A Bar of Mottled Soap.
'A fact so dread,' he faintly said,
   'Extinguishes all hope!'

# Dahn the Plug'ole

## Anon

A muvver was barfin' 'er biby one night,
The youngest of ten and a tiny young mite,
The muvver was pore and the biby was thin,
Only a skellington covered in skin;
The muvver turned rahnd for the soap orf the rack,
She was but a moment, but when she turned back,
The biby was gorn; and in anguish she cried,
'Oh, where is my biby?' – The angels replied:
   'Your biby 'as fell dahn the plug'ole,
'Your biby 'as gorn dahn the plug;
'The poor little thing was so skinny and thin
'E oughter been barfed in a jug;
'Your biby is perfeckly 'appy,
'E won't need a barf any more,
Your biby 'as fell dahn the plug'ole,
Not lorst, but gorn before.'


# The Greedy Cannibal

## Samuel Wilberforce

If I were a Cassowary
   On the plains of Timbuctoo,
I would eat a missionary,
   Cassock, bands, and hymn-book, too.

# Central Eating

## Anon

Radi was a circus lion,
Radi was a woman hater,
Radi had a lady trainer,
Radiator.

# The Greedy Boy

## Anon

The boy stood in the supper-room
Whence all but he had fled;
He'd eaten seven pots of jam
And he was gorged with bread.

'Oh, one more crust before I bust!'
He cried in accents wild;
He licked the plates, he sucked the spoons
He was a vulgar child.

There came a burst of thunder-sound —
The boy — oh! where was he?
Ask of the maid who mopped him up,
The breadcrumbs and the tea!

# The Last Laugh

## Oliver Wendell Holmes

I wrote some lines once on a time
   In wondrous merry mood,
And thought, as usual, men would say
   They were exceeding good.

They were so queer, so very queer,
   I laughed as I would die;
Albeit, in the general way,
   A sober man am I.

I called my servant, and he came;
   How kind it was of him
To mind a slender man like me,
   He of the mighty limb!

'These to the printer,' I exclaimed,
   And, in my humorous way,
I added (as a trifling jest)
   'There'll be the devil to pay.'

He took the paper, and I watched,
   And saw him peep within;
At the first line he read, his face
   Was all upon the grin.

He read the next; the grin grew broad,
    And shot from ear to ear;
He read the third; a chuckling noise
    I now began to hear.

The fourth; he broke into a roar;
    The fifth; his waistband split;
The sixth; he burst five buttons off,
    And tumbled in a fit.

Ten days and nights, with sleepless eye,
    I watched that wretched man,
And since, I never dare to write
    As funny as I can.

## Swan Song

### Samuel Taylor Coleridge

Swans sing before they die – 'twere no bad thing
Should certain persons die before they sing.

# Catching the Cat

Margaret Vandergrift

The mice had met in council,
   They all looked haggard and worn,
For affairs had become too terrible
   To be any longer borne.
Not a family out of mourning –
   There was a crape on every hat.
They were desperate – something must be done,
   And done at once, to the cat.

An elderly member rose and said:
   'It might prove a possible thing
To set the trap which they set for us –
   That one with the awful spring!'
The suggestion was applauded
   Loudly by one and all,
Till somebody squeaked, 'That trap would be
   About ninety-four times too small!'

Then a medical mouse suggested –
   A little under his breath –
They should confiscate the very first mouse
   That died a natural death,
And he'd undertake to poison the cat,
   If they'd let him prepare that mouse.
'There's not been a natural death,' they cried,
   'Since the cat came into the house!'

The smallest mouse in the council
   Arose with a solemn air,
And, by way of increasing his stature,
   Rubbed up his whiskers and hair.
He waited until there was silence
   All along the pantry shelf,
And then he said with dignity:
   'I will catch that cat myself!
When next I hear her coming,
   Instead of running away,
I shall turn and face her boldly,
   And pretend to be at play;
She will not see her danger,
   Poor creature! I suppose;
But as she stoops to catch me,
   I shall catch her, by the nose!'

The mice began to look hopeful,
   Yes, even the old ones; when
A grey-haired sage said slowly,
   'And what will you do with her then?'
The champion, disconcerted,
   Replied with dignity: 'Well,
I think, if you'll excuse me,
   'Twill be wiser not to tell!
We all have our inspirations –'
   This produced a general smirk –
'But we are not all at liberty
   To explain just how they'll work.
I ask you, then, to trust me;
   You need have no further fears –
Consider our enemy done for!' –
   The council gave three cheers.

'I do believe she is coming!'
  Said a small mouse nervously.
'Run if you like,' said the champion,
  'But I shall wait and see!'
And sure enough she was coming –
  The mice all scampered away,
Except the noble champion,
  Who had made up his mind to stay.

The mice had faith, of course they had –
    They were all of them noble souls,
But a sort of general feeling
    Kept them safely in their holes,
Until some time in the evening;
    Then the boldest ventured out,
And saw in the hazy distance
    The cat prance gaily about!

There was dreadful consternation,
    Till some one at last said, 'Oh,
He's not had time to do it,
    Let us not prejudge him so!'
'I believe in him, of course I do,'
    Said the nervous mouse with a sigh,
'But the cat looks suspiciously happy,
    And I wish I did know why!'

The cat, I regret to acknowledge,
    Still prances about that house,
And no message, letter, or telegram
    Has come from the champion mouse.
The mice are a little discouraged,
    The demand for crape goes on;
They feel they'd be happier if they knew
    Where the champion mouse has gone.

This story has a moral –
    It is very short you'll see;
So, of course, you will listen to it,
    For fear of offending me.
It is well to be courageous
    And valiant and all that,
But – if you are mice – you'd better think twice
    Ere you try to catch the cat.

# *Way Down South*

## Anon

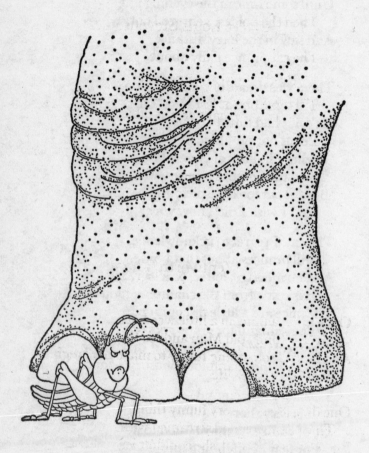

Way down South where bananas grow,
A grasshopper stepped on an elephant's toe,
The elephant said, with tears in his eyes,
'Pick on somebody your own size!'

# The Whole Duty of Children

Robert Louis Stevenson

A child should always say what's true,
And speak when he is spoken to,
And behave mannerly at table:
At least as far as he is able.


# Once Upon a Time

D'Arcy Wentworth Thompson

Once upon a time, in a little wee house,
   Lived a funny old Man and his Wife;
And he said something funny to make her laugh
   Every day of his life.

One day he said a very funny thing,
   That she shook and screamed with laughter;
But the poor old soul, she couldn't leave off
   For at least three whole days after.

# The Pobble who has no Toes

Edward Lear

The Pobble who has no toes
   Had once as many as we;
When they said, 'Some day you may lose them all';
   He replied, – 'Fish fiddle de-dee!'
And his Aunt Jobiska made him drink,
Lavender water tinged with pink,
For she said, 'The World in general knows
There's nothing so good for a Pobble's toes!'

The Pobble who has no toes,
   Swam across the Bristol Channel;
But before he set out he wrapped his nose,
   In a piece of scarlet flannel.
For his Aunt Jobiska said, 'No harm
Can come to his toes if his nose is warm;
And it's perfectly known that a Pobble's toes
Are safe,– provided he minds his nose.'

The Pobble swam fast and well,
   And when boats or ships came near him
He tinkledy-binkledy-winkled a bell,
   So that all the world could hear him.
And all the Sailors and Admirals cried,
When they saw him nearing the further side,
'He has gone to fish, for his Aunt Jobiska's
Runcible Cat with crimson whiskers!'

But before he touched the shore,
   The shore of the Bristol Channel,
A sea-green Porpoise carried away
   His wrapper of scarlet flannel.
And when he came to observe his feet,
Formerly garnished with toes so neat,
His face at once became forlorn
On perceiving that all his toes were gone!

And nobody ever knew
   From that dark day to the present,
Whoso had taken the Pobble's toes,
   In a manner so far from pleasant.
Whether the shrimps or crawfish grey,
Or crafty mermaids stole them away —
Nobody knew; and nobody knows
How the Pobble was robbed of his twice five toes.

The Pobble who has no toes
   Was placed in a friendly Bark,
And they rowed him back, and carried him up,
   To his Aunt Jobiska's Park.
And she made him a feast at his earnest wish
Of eggs and buttercups fried with fish; —
And she said, — 'It's a fact the whole world knows,
That Pobbles are happier without their toes.'

# Life Story

## Anon


Once – but no matter when –
   There lived – no matter where –
A man, whose name – but then
   I need not that declare.

He – well, he had been born,
   And so he was alive;
His age – I details scorn –
   Was somethingty and five.

He lived – how many years
   I truly can't decide;
But this one fact appears
   He lived – until he died.

'He died,' I have averred,
   But cannot prove 'twas so,
But that he was interred,
   At any rate, I know.

I fancy he'd a son,
   I hear he had a wife:
Perhaps he'd more than one,
   I know not, on my life!

But whether he was rich,
   Or whether he was poor,
Or neither – both – or which,
   I cannot say, I'm sure.

I can't recall his name,
   Or what he used to do:
But then — well, such is fame!
   'Twill so serve me and you.


And that is why I thus,
   About this unknown man
Would fain create a fuss,
   To rescue, if I can.


From dark oblivion's blow,
   Some record of his lot:
But, ah! I do not know
   Who — where — when — why — or what.


## The Crooked Crook

Anon


Forth from his den to steal he stole,
His bag of chink he chunk,
And many a wicked smile he smole,
And many a wink he wunk.

47

# There Lived an Old Man

D'Arcy Wentworth Thompson

There lived an old man in a garret,
    So afraid of a little tom-cat,
That he pulled himself up to the ceiling,
    And hung himself up in his hat.

And for fear of the wind and the rain
    He took his umbrella to bed –
I've half an idea that silly old man
    Was a little bit wrong in his head.

# Greedy Richard

## Jane Taylor

'I think I want some pies this morning,'
Said Dick, stretching himself and yawning.
So down he threw his slate and books,
And sauntered to the pastry cook's.

And there he cast his greedy eyes
Round on the jellies and the pies,
So to select with anxious care
The very nicest that was there.

At last the point was well decided –
As his opinion was divided
'Twixt pie and jelly, being loth
Either to leave – he took them both.

Now Richard never could be pleased
To stop when hunger was appeased;
But would go on to eat still more
Though he had had an ample store.

'No, not another now,' said Dick,
'Dear me! I feel extremely sick.
I cannot even eat this bit.
I wish – I – had not – tasted – it.'

Then slowly rising from his seat
He threw his cheesecake in the street,
And left the tempting pastry-cook's
With very discontented looks.

49

# The Whango Tree

## Anon

The woggly bird sat on the whango tree,
   Nooping the rinkum corn,
And graper and graper, alas! grew he,
   And cursed the day he was born.
His crute was clum and his voice was rum,
   As curiously thur sang he,
'Oh, would I'd been rammed and eternally
      clammed
Ere I perched on this whango tree.'

Now the whango tree had a bubbly thorn,
   As sharp as a nootie's bill,
And it stuck in the woggly bird's umptum lorn
   And weepadge, the smart did thrill.
He fumbled and cursed, but that wasn't the worst,
   For he couldn't at all get free,
And he cried, 'I am gammed, and injustibly
      named
On the luggardly whango tree.'

And there he sits still, with no worm in his bill,
   Nor no guggledom in his nest;
He is hungry and bare, and gobliddered with care,
   And his grabbles give him no rest;
He is weary and sore and his tugmut is raw
   And nothing to nob has he,
As he chirps, 'I am blammed and corruptibly
      jammed,
In this cuggerdom whango tree.'

# An Accident

Anon

An accident happened to my brother Jim
When somebody threw a tomato at him —
Tomatoes are juicy and don't hurt the skin,
But this one was specially packed in a tin.

# Skewe-wiff!

### Anon

A railway official of Skewe
Met an engine one day that he knew.
   Though he smiled and he bowed,
   That engine was proud;
It cut him – it cut him in two!


# The Old Fellow of Lympne

### Anon

There was an old fellow of Lympne,
Who said, 'How I wish I was slim!'
   So he lived for three weeks
   On a nut and two leeks
And that was the last heard of him.

# The Young Man of Devizes

## Anon

There was a young man of Devizes,
Whose ears were of different sizes;
    One was quite small,
    And of no use at all,
But the other was huge and won prizes.

# The Cheerful Old Bear

Anon

A cheerful old bear at the Zoo
Could always find something to do.
    When it bored him, you know,
    To walk to and fro,
He reversed it, and walked fro and to.

# Cold Apple Pies

## Anon

I loathe, abhor, detest, despise,
Abominate cold apple pies.
I like good bread, I like good meat,
Or anything that's fit to eat;
But of all poor grub beneath the
   skies,
The poorest is cold apple pies.
Give me the toothache, or sore
   eyes,
But don't give me cold apple pies.
The farmer takes his gnarliest fruit,
'Tis wormy, bitter, and hard, to
   boot;
He leaves the hulls to make us
   cough,
And don't take half the peeling off.
Then on a dirty cord 'tis strung
And in a garret window hung,
And there it serves as roost for
   flies,
Until it's made up into pies.
Tread on my corns, or tell me lies,
But don't pass me cold apple pies.

# Monkey Nuts

Anon

Well I never, did you ever,
See a monkey dressed in leather?
Leather eyes, leather nose,
Leather breeches to his toes.


# Mad Midnight

Anon

'Tis midnight, and the setting sun
Is slowly rising in the west;
The rapid rivers slowly run,
The frog is on his downy nest.
The pensive goat and sportive cow,
Hilarious, leap from bough to bough.

# The Old Man of Dunoon

Anon

There was an old man of Dunoon
Who always ate soup with a fork.
   For he said: 'As I eat
    Neither fish, fowl, nor flesh,
I should otherwise finish too quick.'

# *Foolish Harriet*

## Heinrich Hoffman

It almost makes me cry to tell
What foolish Harriet befell.
Mamma and Nurse went out one day
And left her all alone at play;
Now, on the table close at hand,
A box of matches chanc'd to stand;
And kind Mamma and Nurse had told her,
That, if she touch'd them, they should scold her,
But Harriet said: 'Oh, what a pity!
For, when they burn, it is so pretty;
They crackle so, and spit, and flame;
Mamma, too, often does the same.'

The pussy-cats heard this,
And they began to hiss,
And stretch their claws
And raise their paws;
'Me-ow,' they said, 'me-ow, me-o,
You'll burn to death, if you do so.'

But Harriet would not take advice,
She lit a match, it was so nice!
It crackled so, it burn'd so clear, –
Exactly like the picture here.
She jumped for joy and ran about
And was too pleas'd to put it out.

The pussy-cats saw this
And said: 'Oh, naughty, naughty Miss!'
And stretch'd their claws
And rais'd their paws:
' 'Tis very, very wrong, you know,
Me-ow, mee-o, me-ow, me-o,
You will be burnt if you do so.'

And see! Oh! what a dreadful thing!
The fire has caught her apron-string;
Her apron burns, her arms, her hair;
She burns all over, everywhere.

Then how the pussy-cats did mew,
What else, poor pussies, could they do?
They scream'd for help, 'twas all in vain!
So then they said: 'We'll scream again;
Make haste, make haste, me-ow, me-o,
She'll burn to death, we told her so.'

So she was burnt, with all her clothes,
And arms, and hands, and eyes, and nose;
Till she had nothing more to lose
Except her little scarlet shoes;
And nothing else but these was found
Among her ashes on the ground.

And when the good cats sat beside
The smoking ashes, how they cried!
'Me-ow, me-oo, me-ow, me-oo,
What will Mamma and Nursy do?'
Their tears ran down their cheeks so fast;
They made a little pond at last.

# The Pessimist

## Ben King

Nothing to do but work,
   Nothing to eat but food,
Nothing to wear but clothes
   To keep one from going nude.

Nothing to breathe but air,
   Quick as a flash 'tis gone;
Nowhere to fall but off,
   Nowhere to stand but on.

Nothing to comb but hair,
   Nowhere to sleep but in bed,
Nothing to weep but tears,
   Nothing to bury but dead.

Nothing to sing but songs,
   Ah, well, alas! alack!
Nowhere to go but out,
   Nowhere to come but back.

Nothing to see but sights,
   Nothing to quench but thirst,
Nothing to have but what we've got;
   Thus thro' life we are cursed.

Nothing to strike but a gait;
   Everything moves that goes.
Nothing at all but common sense
   Can ever withstand these woes.

# Mr Finney's Turnip

## Anon

Mr Finney had a turnip
  And it grew and it grew;
And it grew behind the barn,
  And that turnip did no harm.

There it grew and it grew
  Till it could grow no longer;
Then his daughter Lizzie picked it
  And put it in the cellar.

There it lay and it lay
  Till it began to rot;
And his daughter Susie took it
  And put it in the pot.

And they boiled it and boiled it
  As long as they were able,
And then his daughters took it
  And put it on the table.

Mr Finney and his wife
  They sat down to sup;
And they ate and they ate
  And they ate that turnip up.

# Utter Nonsense

### Harriet White

When sporgles spanned the floreate mead
   And cogwogs gleet upon the lea,
Uffia gopped to meet her love
   Who smeeged upon the equat sea.

Dately she walked aglost the sand;
   The boreal wind seet in her face;
The moggling waves yalped at her feet;
   Pangwangling was her pace.

# On the Bridge

### Anon

He stood on the bridge at midnight,
Disturbing my sweet repose,
For he was a large mosquito –
And the bridge was the bridge of my nose!

# Old Mother Hubbard

Sarah Catherine Martin

Old Mother Hubbard
Went to the cupboard,
To fetch her poor dog a bone;
But when she got there
The cupboard was bare,
And so the poor dog had none.

She went to the baker's
To buy him some bread;
But when she came back
The poor dog was dead.

She went to the undertaker's
To buy him a coffin;
But when she came back
The poor dog was laughin'.

She took a clean dish
To get him some tripe;
But when she came back
He was smoking a pipe.

She went to the alehouse
To get him some beer;
But when she came back
The dog sat in a chair.

She went to the tavern
    For wine white and red;
But when she came back
    The dog stood on his head.

She went to the fruiterer's
    To buy him some fruit;
But when she came back
    He was playing the flute.

64

She went to the tailor's
    To buy him a coat;
But when she came back
    He was riding a goat.

She went to the hatter's,
    To buy him a hat;
But when she came back
    He was feeding the cat.

She went to the barber's
    To buy him a wig;
But when she came back
    He was dancing a jig.

She went to the cobbler's
    To buy him some shoes;
But when she came back
    He was reading the news.

She went to the seamstress
    To buy him some linen;
But when she came back
    The dog was a-spinnin'.

She went to the hosier's
    To buy him some hose;
But when she came back
    He was dressed in his clothes.

The dame made a curtsy,
    The dog made a bow;
The dame said: 'Your servant.'
    The dog said: 'Bow-wow!'

# Epitaph for John Bun

### Anon

Here lies John Bun,
He was killed by a gun,
His name was not Bun, but Wood,
But Wood would not rhyme with gun, but Bun would.


# The Missing Punctuation

### Anon

Caesar entered on his head
A helmet on each foot
A sandal in his hand he had
His trusty sword to boot.

# The Walrus and the Carpenter

## Lewis Carroll

The sun was shining on the sea,
   Shining with all his might:
He did his very best to make
   The billows smooth and bright –
And this was odd, because it was
   The middle of the night.

The moon was shining sulkily,
   Because she thought the sun
Had got no business to be there
   After the day was done –
'It's very rude of him,' she said,
   'To come and spoil the fun!'

The sea was wet as wet could be,
   The sands were dry as dry.
You could not see a cloud, because
   No cloud was in the sky:
No birds were flying overhead –
   There were no birds to fly.

The Walrus and the Carpenter
   Were walking close at hand:
They wept like anything to see
   Such quantities of sand:
'If this were only cleared away,'
   They said, 'it would be grand!'

'If seven maids with seven mops
    Swept it for half a year,
Do you suppose,' the Walrus said,
    'That they could get it clear?'
'I doubt it,' said the Carpenter,
    And shed a bitter tear.

'O Oysters, come and walk with us!'
    The Walrus did beseech.
'A pleasant walk, a pleasant talk,
    Along the briny beach:
We cannot do with more than four,
    To give a hand to each.'

The eldest Oyster looked at him,
    But not a word he said:
The eldest Oyster winked his eye,
    And shook his heavy head –
Meaning to say he did not choose
    To leave the oyster-bed.

But four young Oysters hurried up,
    All eager for the treat:
Their coats were brushed, their faces washed,
    Their shoes were clean and neat –
And this was odd, because, you know,
    They hadn't any feet.

Four other Oysters followed them,
    And yet another four;
And thick and fast they came at last,
    And more, and more, and more –
All hopping through the frothy waves,
    And scrambling to the shore.

The Walrus and the Carpenter
    Walked on a mile or so,
And then they rested on a rock
    Conveniently low:
And all the little Oysters stood
    And waited in a row.

'The time has come,' the Walrus said,
    'To talk of many things:
Of shoes – and ships – and sealing wax –
    Of cabbages – and kings –
And why the sea is boiling hot –
    And whether pigs have wings.'

'But wait a bit,' the Oysters cried,
    'Before we have our chat;
For some of us are out of breath,
    And all of us are fat!'
'No hurry!' said the Carpenter.
    They thanked him much for that.

'A loaf of bread,' the Walrus said,
    'Is what we chiefly need:
Pepper and vinegar besides
    Are very good indeed –
Now, if you're ready, Oysters, dear,
    We can begin to feed.'

'But not on us!' the Oysters cried,
    Turning a little blue.
'After such kindness that would be
    A dismal thing to do!'
'The night is fine,' the Walrus said,
    'Do you admire the view?

'It was so kind of you to come,
    And you are very nice!'
The Carpenter said nothing but
    'Cut us another slice.
I wish you were not quite so deaf —
    I've had to ask you twice!'

'It seems a shame,' the Walrus said,
    'To play them such a trick.
After we've brought them out so far,
    And made them trot so quick!'
The Carpenter said nothing but
    'The butter's spread too thick!'

'I weep for you,' the Walrus said:
    'I deeply sympathise.'
With sobs and tears he sorted out
    Those of the largest size,
Holding his pocket-handkerchief
    Before his streaming eyes.

'O Oysters,' said the Carpenter,
    'You've had a pleasant run!
Shall we be trotting home again?'
    But answer came there none —
And this was scarcely odd, because
    They'd eaten every one.

# If You Should Meet a Crocodile

## Anon

If you should meet a crocodile,
  Don't take a stick and poke him;
Ignore the welcome in his smile,
  Be careful not to stroke him.
For as he sleeps upon the Nile,
  He thinner gets and thinner;
And whene'er you meet a crocodile
  He's ready for his dinner.

# Food for Thought

Anon

Through the teeth
And past the gums –
Look out stomach,
Here it comes!

# Catastrophe

Anon

There were once two cats of Kilkenny,
Each thought there was one cat too many;
So they fought and they fit,
And they scratched and they bit,
Till, excepting their nails
And the tips of their tails,
Instead of two cats, there weren't any.

# The Policeman's Lot

## W. S. Gilbert

When a felon's not engaged in his employment–
Or maturing his felonious little plans –
His capacity for innocent enjoyment –
Is just as great as any honest man's –
Our feelings we with difficulty smother –
When constabulary duty's to be done –
Ah, take one consideration with another –
The policeman's lot is not a happy one.
    When constabulary duty's to be done –
     To be done,
     The policeman's lot is not a happy one.

When the enterprising burglar's not a-burgling –
When the cut-throat isn't occupied in crime –
He loves to hear the little brook a-gurgling –
And listen to the merry village chime –
When the coster's finished jumping on his mother –
He loves to lie a-basking in the sun –
Ah, take one consideration with another –
The policeman's lot is not a happy one.
    When constabulary duty's to be done –
     To be done,
     The policeman's lot is not a happy one –
     Happy one.

# The Elderly Gentleman

## George Canning

By the side of a murmuring stream an elderly
  gentleman sat.
On the top of his head was a wig, and a-top
  of his wig was his hat.

The wind it blew high and blew strong, as the
  elderly gentleman sat;
And bore from his head in a trice, and plunged in
  river his hat.

The gentleman then took his cane which lay by
  his side as he sat;
And he dropped in the river his wig, in attempting
  to get out his hat.

His breast it grew cold with despair, and full in his
  eye madness sat;
So he flung in the river his cane to swim with his
  wig and his hat.

Cool reflection at last came across while this
  elderly gentleman sat;
So he thought he would follow the stream and look
  for his cane, wig, and hat.

His head being thicker than common, o'er-balanced
  the rest of his fat;
And in plumped this son of a woman to follow his
  wig, cane, and hat.

# The Tibetan Elephant

## Anon

An elephant born in Tibet,
One day in its cage wouldn't get.
  So its keeper stood near
  Stuck a hose in its ear,
And invented the first Jumbo Jet.

# Do Not Spit

Anon

There was an old man of Darjeeling
Who travelled from London to Ealing
   It said on the door,
    'Please don't spit on the floor,'
So he carefully spat on the ceiling.

# The Young Lady of Lynn

Anon

There was a young lady of Lynn,
Who was so uncommonly thin,
   That when she essayed
   To drink lemonade,
She slipped through the straw and fell in.

# Ned

## Anon

There was a young person named Ned
Who dined before going to bed,
  On lobster and ham
  And salad and jam,
And when he awoke he was dead.

# Sue

## Anon

There was a young woman named Sue,
Who wanted to catch the 2:02;
  Said the trainman, 'Don't hurry
  Or flurry or worry;
It's a minute or two to 2:02.'

# No!

## Thomas Hood

No sun – no moon!
No morn – no noon –
No dawn – no dusk – no proper time of day –
No sky – no earthly view –
No distance looking blue –
No road – no street – no 't'other side the way'
No end to any Row –
No indications where the Crescents go –
No top to any steeple –
No recognitions of familiar people –
No courtesies for showing 'em –
No knowing 'em! –
No travelling at all – no locomotion,
No inkling of the way – no notion –
'No go' – by land or ocean –
No mail – no post –
No news from any foreign coast –
No Park – no Ring – no afternoon gentility –
No company – no nobility –
No warmth, no cheerfulness, no healthful ease,
No comfortable feel in any member –
No shade, no shine, no butterflies, no bees,
No fruits, no flowers, no leaves, no birds, –
November!

# The Dong with a Luminous Nose

### Edward Lear

When awful darkness and silence reign
Over the great Grombolian plain,
Through the long, long wintry nights; –
  When the angry breakers roar
  As they beat on the rocky shore; –
When Storm-clouds brood on the towering heights
Of the Hills of the Chankly Bore: –

Then, through the vast and gloomy dark,
There moves what seems a fiery spark,
A lonely spark with silvery rays
        Piercing the coal-black night, –
        A meteor strange and bright: –
Hither and thither the vision strays,
A single lurid light.

Slowly it wanders, – pauses, – creeps, –
Anon it sparkles, – flashes and leaps;
And ever as onward it gleaming goes
A light on the Bong-tree stems it throws.
And those who watch at that midnight hour
From Hall or Terrace, or lofty Tower,
Cry, as the wild light passes along, –
      'The Dong! – the Dong!
   'The wandering Dong through the forest goes!
      'The Dong! the Dong!
   'The Dong with a luminous Nose!'

      Long years ago
   The Dong was happy and gay,
Till he fell in love with a Jumbly Girl
Who came to those shores one day

For the Jumblies came in a Sieve, they did, –
Landing at eve near the Zemmery Fidd
    Where the Oblong Oysters grow,
      And the rocks are smooth and grey.

And all the woods and the valleys rang
With the Chorus they daily and nightly sang, –
    'Far and few, far and few,
      Are the lands where the Jumblies live;
      Their heads are green, and their hands are blue
      And they went to sea in a sieve.'

Happily, happily passed those days!
While the cheerful Jumblies stayed
They danced in circlets all night long,
To the plaintive pipe of the lively Dong,
In moonlight, shine, or shade.

For day and night he was always there
By the side of the Jumbly Girl so fair,
With her sky-blue hands, and her sea-green hair.
Till the morning came of that hateful day
When the Jumblies sailed in their sieve away,
When the Dong was left on the cruel shore
Gazing – gazing for evermore, –
Ever keeping his weary eyes on
That pea-green sail on the far horizon, –
Singing the Jumbly Chorus still
As he sat all day on the grassy hill, –
    'Far and few, far and few,
    Are the lands where the Jumblies live;
    Their heads are green, and their hands are blue,
    And they went to sea in a sieve.'

But when the sun was low in the West,
    The Dong arose and said, –
'What little sense I once possessed
    Has quite gone out of my head!'

And since that day he wanders still
By lake and forest, marsh and hill,
Singing – 'O somewhere, in valley or plain
'Might I find my Jumbly Girl again!
'For ever I'll seek by lake and shore
'Till I find my Jumbly Girl once more!'
Playing a pipe with silvery squeaks,

Since then his Jumbly Girl he seeks,
And because by night he could not see,
He gathered the bark of the Twangum Tree
On the flowery plain that grows
   And he wove him a wondrous Nose, –
   A Nose as strange as a Nose could be!
Of vast proportions and painted red,
And tied with cords to the back of his head.
–In a hollow rounded space it ended
With a luminous lamp within suspended,
   All fenced about
   With a bandage stout
   To prevent the wind from blowing it out;
And with holes all round to send the light,
In gleaming rays on the dismal night.

And now each night, and all night long,
Over those plains still roams the Dong;
And above the wail of the Chimp and Snipe
You may hear the squeak of his plaintive pipe
While ever he seeks, but seeks in vain
To meet with his Jumbly Girl again;
Lonely and wild – all night he goes, –
The Dong with a luminous Nose!
And all who watch at the midnight hour,
From Hall or Terrace, or lofty Tower,
Cry, as they trace the Meteor bright,
Moving along through the dreary night,–
   'This is the hour when forth he goes,
   'The Dong with a luminous Nose!
   'Yonder – over the plain he goes;
     'He goes;
     'He goes;
(The Dong with a luminous Nose!'

# *Drink and Be Merry!*

## Anon

The horse and mule live thirty years
And nothing know of wines and beers.
The goat and sheep at twenty die
And never taste of Scotch or Rye.
The cow drinks water by the ton
And at eighteen is mostly done.
The dog at eleven cashes in
Without the aid of rum and gin.
The cat in milk and water soaks
And then in twelve short years it croaks.
The modest, sober, bone-dry hen
Lays eggs for nogs, then dies at ten,
All animals are strictly dry:
They sinless live and swiftly die;
But sinful, ginful, rum-soaked men
Survive for three score years and ten.
And some of them, a very few,
Stay pickled till they're ninety-two.

# *Oh, the Train*

## Anon

Oh, the train pulled in the station.
  The bell was ringing wet.
The track ran by the depot,
  And I think it's running yet.

'Twas midnight on the ocean.
  Not a streetcar was in sight.
The sun and moon were shining.
  And it rained all day that night.

'Twas a summer day in winter,
  And the snow was raining fast
As a barefoot boy with shoes on
  Stood sitting on the grass.

Oh, I jumped into the river
  Just because it had a bed.
I took a sheet of water
  For to cover up my head.

Oh, the rain makes all things
      beautiful,
  The flowers and grasses, too.
If the rain makes all things
      beautiful,
  Why don't it rain on you?

# Diddle Diddle Dumpling

Anon

Diddle diddle dumpling, my son John,
Ate a pasty five feet long;
He bit it once, he bit it twice,
Oh, my goodness, it was full of mice!

# Fisherman on Toast

## Edward Abbott Parry

The Sardine was lurking behind in the tin
  To smooth his young whiskers in oil,
Whilst his sister was fanning the flames with her fin
  In hopes that the kettle would boil.
The Shrimp and the Pilchard had changed a bank-note
  To pay the old Salmon his debt,
When the black-hearted fisherman came in his boat
  And scooped up the lot in his net.

The callow young Bloater was darning a frill,
    The Gurnet was trolling for grouse,
The Lobster was mildly dissuading the Brill
    From the folly of building a house.
The Mackerel was tossing about in his bed
    And dreaming of parsley and cooks,
And the black-hearted fisherman smiled as he said:
    'I can catch all these fellows on hooks!'

A Storm-Cloud the size of an extra large bat
    Came walloping out of the west,
He was thick as a waterproof, black as a hat,
    And he hugged the cold hail to his breast.
He burst o'er the black-hearted fisherman's head
    When he caught him five miles from the coast,
Then the kind-hearted Cloud as he got into bed
Rejoiced that those dear little fishes were fed
    On fisherman served up on toast.

## Three Wise Men

Anon

Three wise men of Gotham,
They went to sea in a bowl,
And if the bowl had been stronger,
My song had been longer.

# If

Anon

If all the land were apple-pie,
And all the sea were ink;
And all the trees were bread and cheese,
What should we do for drink?

# Peter Prim

Anon

'Peter Prim! Peter Prim!
Why do you in stockings swim?'
Peter Prim gave this reply,
'To make such fools as you ask why!'

# The Hare and the Tortoise

Anon

A rabbit raced a turtle,
You know the turtle won;
And Mister Bunny came in late,
A little hot cross bun!

# To a Fish

### Peter Pindar

Enjoy thy stream, O harmless fish;
And when an angler for his dish,
   Through gluttony's vile sin,
Attempts, a wretch, to pull thee out,
God give thee strength, O gentle trout,
   To pull the rascal in!

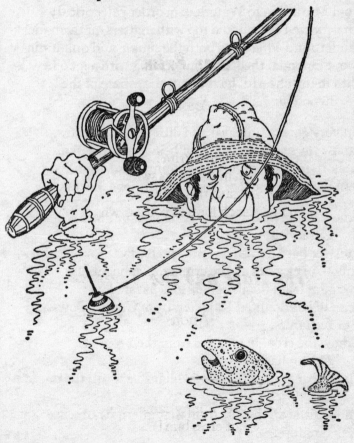

# The Modern Major-General

## W. S. Gilbert

I am the very model of a modern Major-General,
I've information vegetable, animal, and mineral,
I know the kings of England, and I quote the fights
    historical,
From Marathon to Waterloo, in order categorical;
I'm very well acquainted too with matters mathematical,
I understand equations, both the simple and quadratical,
About binomial theorem I'm teeming with a lot o'news —
With many cheerful facts about the square of the
    hypotenuse.

I'm very good at integral and differential calculus,
I know the scientific names of beings animalculous;
In short, in matters vegetable, animal, and mineral,
I am the very model of a modern Major-General.

I know our mythic history, King Arthur's and Sir
    Caradoc's,
I answer hard acrostics, I've a pretty taste for paradox,
I quote in elegiacs all the crimes of Heliogabalus,
In conics I can floor peculiarities parabolous.
I can tell undoubted Raphaels from Gerard Dows and
    Zoffanies,
I know the croaking chorus from the Frogs of
    Aristophanes,
Then I can hum a fugue of which I've heard the music's
    din afore,
And whistle all the airs from that infernal nonsense
    Pinafore.

Then I can write a washing bill in Babylonic cuneiform,
And tell you every detail of Caractacus's uniform;
In short, in matters vegetable, animal, and mineral,
I am the very model of a modern Major-General.

In fact, when I know what is meant by 'mamelon' and
 'ravelin',
When I can tell at sight a chassepot rifle from a javelin,
When such affairs as sorties and surprises I'm more wary
 at,
And when I know precisely what is meant by
 'commissariat',
When I have learnt what progress has been made in
 modern gunnery,
When I know more of tactics than a novice in a nunnery;
In short, when I've a smattering of elemental strategy,
You'll say a better Major-General has never sat a gee —
For my military knowledge, though I'm plucky and
 adventury,
Has only been brought down to the beginning of the
 century;
But still in matters vegetable, animal, and mineral,
I am the very model of a modern Major-General.

# A Cat's Conscience

Anon

A Dog will often steal a bone,
But conscience lets him not alone,
And by his tail his guilt is known.

But Cats consider theft a game,
And, howsoever you may blame,
Refuse the slightest sign of shame.

When food mysteriously goes,
The chances are that Pussy knows
More than she leads you to suppose.

And hence there is no need for you,
If Puss declines a meal or two,
To feel her pulse and make ado.


# Have you Heard?

Anon

Have you heard of the man
    Who stood on his head,
And put his clothes
    Into his bed,
And folded himself
    On a chair instead?

# There was a Little Girl

Henry Wadsworth Longfellow

There was a little girl,
And she had a little curl
   Right in the middle of her forehead.
When she was good
She was very, very good,
   And when she was bad she was horrid.

One day she went upstairs,
When her parents, unawares,
   In the kitchen were occupied with meals
And she stood upon her head
In her little trundle-bed,
   And then began hooraying with her heels.

Her mother heard the noise,
And she thought it was the boys
   A-playing at a combat in the attic;
But when she climbed the stair,
And found Jemima there,
   She took and she did spank her most emphatic.

# The Jumblies

## Edward Lear

They went to sea in a Sieve, they did,
   In a Sieve they went to sea;
In spite of all their friends could say,
On a winter's morn, on a stormy day,
   In a Sieve they went to sea!
And when the Sieve turned round and round,
And everyone cried, 'You'll all be drowned!'
They called aloud, 'Our Sieve ain't big,
But we don't care a button, we don't care a fig!
   In a Sieve we'll go to sea.'

     Far and few, far and few,
       Are the lands where the Jumblies live;
       Their heads are green, and their hands are blue,
        And they went to sea in a Sieve.

They sailed away in a Sieve, they did,
   In a Sieve they sailed so fast;
With only a beautiful pea-green veil
Tied with a riband by way of a sail
   To a small tobacco-pipe mast;
And everyone said, who saw them go,
'O won't they be soon upset, you know,
For the sky is dark, and the voyage is long,
And happen what may, it's extremely wrong,
   In a Sieve to sail so fast.'

     Far and few, far and few,
       Are the lands where the Jumblies live;
       Their heads are green, and their hands are blue,
        And they went to sea in a Sieve.

The water it soon came in, it did,
    The water it soon came in;
So to keep them dry, they wrapped their feet
In a pinky paper, all folded neat,
    And they fastened it down with a pin.
And they passed the night in a crockery jar,
And each of them said, 'How wise we are!
Though the sky be dark and the voyage be long
Yet we never can think we were rash or wrong,
    While round in our Sieve we spin!'

        Far and few, far and few,
            Are the lands where the Jumblies live;
        Their heads are green, and their hands are blue,
            And they went to sea in a Sieve.

And all night long they sailed away;
    And when the sun went down,
They whistled and warbled a moony song,
To the echoing sound of a coppery gong,
    In the shade of the mountains brown.
'O Timballo! How happy we are,
When we live in a Sieve and a crockery jar,
And all night long in the moonlight pale,
We sail away with a pea-green sail
    In the shade of the mountains brown!'

        Far and few, far and few,
            Are the lands where the Jumblies live;
        Their heads are green, and their hands are blue,
            And they went to sea in a Sieve.

They sailed to the Western Sea, they did,
  To a land all covered with trees,
And they bought an Owl and a useful Cart,
And a pound of Rice and a Cranberry Tart,
  And a hive of silvery Bees.
And they bought a Pig, and some green Jack-daws,
And a lovely Monkey with lollipop paws,
And forty bottles of Ring-Bo-Ree,
  And no end of Stilton Cheese.

    Far and few, far and few,
      Are the lands where the Jumblies live;
    Their heads are green, and their hands are blue,
      And they went to sea in a Sieve.

And in twenty years they all came back,
  In twenty years or more.
And everyone said, 'How tall they've grown!
For they've been to the Lakes, and the Torrible Zone,
  And the hills of the Chankly Bore';
And they drank their health and gave them a feast
Of dumplings made of beautiful yeast;
And everyone said, 'If we only live,
We too, will go to sea in a Sieve –
  To the hills of the Chankly Bore!'

    Far and few, far and few,
      Are the lands where the Jumblies live;
    Their heads are green, and their hands are blue,
      And they went to sea in a Sieve.

# Fife Folk

## Anon

In a cottage in Fife
Lived a man and his wife,
Who, believe me, were comical folk;
For, to people's surprise,
They both saw with their eyes,
And their tongues moved whenever they spoke!
When quite fast asleep,
I've been told that to keep
Their eyes open they could not contrive;
And they walked on their feet,
And 'twas thought what they eat
Helped, with drinking, to keep them alive!

# The Fleas

## A. de Morgan

Great fleas have little fleas upon their backs to bite 'em,
And little fleas have lesser fleas and so ad infinitum.
And the great fleas themselves, in turn, have greater fleas
   to go on;
While these again have greater still, and greater still, and
   so on.

# The Man and the Hare

## Heinrich Hoffman

This is the man that shoots the hares;
This is the coat he always wears:
With game-bag, powder-horn and gun
He's going out to have some fun.

The hare sits snug in leaves and grass,
And laughs to see the green man pass.

He finds it hard, without a pair
Of spectacles, to shoot the hare.

Now, as the sun grew very hot,
And he a heavy gun had got,
He lay down underneath a tree
And went to sleep as you may see.

And, while he slept like any top,
The little hare came, hop, hop, hop,
Took gun and spectacles, and then
On her hind legs went off again.

The green man wakes and sees her place
 The spectacles upon her face;
And now she's trying all she can
To shoot the sleepy, green-coat man.
He cries and screams and runs away;
The hare runs after him all day,
And hears him call out everywhere:
'Help! Fire! Help! The Hare! The Hare!'

At last he stumbled at the well
Head over ears, and in he fell.
The hare stopp'd short, took aim, and hark!
Bang went the gun, – she miss'd her mark!
The poor man's wife was drinking up
Her coffee in her coffee-cup;
The gun shot cup and saucer through:
'O dear!' cried she, 'What shall I do?'
There liv'd close by the cottage there
The hare's own child, the little hare;
And while she stood upon her toes,
The coffee fell and burn'd her nose.
'O dear!' she cried, with spoon in hand,
'Such fun I do not understand.'


# Rhyme for a Simpleton

## Anon

I said, 'This horse, sir, will you shoe?'
    And soon the horse was shod.
I said, 'This deed, sir, will you do?'
    And soon the deed was dod!

I said, "This stick, sir, will you break?
    At once the stick he broke.
I said, 'This coat, sir, will you make?'
    And soon the coat he moke!

# As

## Anon

As wet as a fish – as dry as a bone;
As live as a bird – as dead as a stone;
As plump as a partridge – as poor as a rat;
As strong as a horse – as weak as a cat;
As hard as a flint – as soft as a mole;
As white as a lily – as black as a coal;
As plain as a pike-staff – as rough as a bear;
As light as a drum – as free as the air;
As heavy as lead – as light as a feather;
As steady as time – uncertain as weather;
As hot as an oven – as cold as a frog;
As gay as a lark – as sick as a dog;
As slow as the tortoise – as swift as the wind;
As true as the Gospel – as false as mankind;
As thin as a herring – as fat as a pig;
As proud as a peacock – as blithe as a grig;
As savage as tigers – as mild as a dove;
As stiff as a poker – as limp as a glove;
As blind as a bat – as deaf as a post;
As cool as a cucumber – as warm as a toast;
As flat as a flounder – as round as a ball;
As blunt as a hammer – as sharp as an awl;
As fierce as a ferret – as safe as the stocks;
As bold as a thief – as sly as a fox;
As straight as an arrow – as crook'd as a bow;
As yellow as saffron – as black as a sloe;
As brittle as glass – as tough as gristle;
As neat as my nail – as clean as a whistle;

As good as a feast – as bad as a witch;
As light as is day – as dark as is pitch;
As brisk as a bee – as dull as an ass;
As full as a tick – as solid as brass.


# *Accidentally*

## Anon

The fable which I now present,
Occurred to me by accident:
And whether bad or excellent,
Is merely so by accident.

A stupid ass this morning went
Into a field by accident:
And cropped his food, and was content,
Until he spied by accident
A flute which some oblivious gent
Had left behind by accident;
When sniffing it with eager scent,
He breathed on it by accident,
And made the hollow instrument
Emit a sound by accident.
'Hurrah, hurrah!' exclaimed the brute,
'How cleverly I play the flute!'

A fool, in spite of nature's bent,
May shine for once, by accident.

# *You are Old, Father William*

## Lewis Carroll

'You are old, Father William,' the young man said,
   'And your hair has become very white;
And yet you incessantly stand on your head –
   Do you think, at your age, it is right?'

'In my youth,' Father William replied to his son,
   'I feared it might injure the brain;
But, now that I'm perfectly sure I have none,
   Why, I do it again and again.'

'You are old,' said the youth, 'as I mentioned before,
   And have grown most uncommonly fat;
Yet you turned a back-somersault in at the door –
   Pray, what is the reason of that?'

'In my youth,' said the sage, as he shook his grey locks,
   'I kept all my limbs very supple
By the use of this ointment – one shilling the box –
   Allow me to sell you a couple?'

'You are old,' said the youth, 'and your jaws are too weak
   For anything rougher than suet;
Yet you finished the goose, with the bones and the beak –
   Pray, how did you manage to do it?'

'In my youth,' said his father, 'I took to the law,
   And argued each case with my wife;
And the muscular strength, which it gave to my jaw,
   Has lasted the rest of my life.'

'You are old,' said the youth, 'one would hardly suppose
    That your eyes was as steady as ever;
Yet you balance an eel on the end of your nose –
    What made you so awfully clever?'

'I have answered three questions, and that is enough,'
    Said his father; 'don't give yourself airs!
Do you think I can listen all day to such stuff?
    Be off, or I'll kick you downstairs!'

## *To Be or Not To Be*

Anon

I sometimes think I'd rather crow
And be a rooster than to roost
And be a crow. But I dunno.

A rooster he can roost also,
Which don't seem fair when crows can't crow.
Which may help some. Still I dunno.

Crows should be glad of one thing, though;
Nobody thinks of eating crow,
While roosters they are good enough
For anyone unless they're tough.

There are lots of tough old roosters though,
And anyway a crow can't crow,
So mebby roosters stand more show.
It looks that way. But I dunno.

# Fishy Tale

## Christina Rossetti

When fishes set umbrellas up
   If the rain-drops run,
Lizards will want their parasols
   To shade them from the sun.

The peacock has a score of eyes,
   With which he cannot see;
The cod-fish has a silent sound,
   However that may be.

No dandelions tell the time,
   Although they turn to clocks,
Cat's cradle does not hold the cat,
   Nor foxglove fit the fox.

# A Tragic Story

## William Makepeace Thackeray

There lived a sage in days of yore,
And he a handsome pigtail wore;
But wondered much and sorrowed more,
Because it hung behind him.

He mused upon this curious case,
And swore he'd changed the pigtail's place
And have it hanging at his face,
Not dangling there behind him.

Says he, 'The mystery I've found, –
I'll turn me round,'
He turned him round;
But still it hung behind him.

Then round and round, and out and in,
All day the puzzled sage did spin;
In vain – it mattered not a pin –
The pigtail hung behind him.

And right, and left, and round about,
And up, and down, and in, and out
He turned; but still the pigtail stout
Hung steadily behind him.

And though his efforts never slack,
And though he twist, and twirl, and tack,
Alas! still faithful to his back,
The pigtail hangs behind him.

# The Two Brothers

## Anon

There was a man who had two sons,
And these two sons were brothers,
And John it was the name of one,
And Charlie was the other's.

Now these two brothers had a shirt,
And it was black and white,
And John he wore it all the day,
And Charlie all the night.

Now these two brothers had a coat,
Of a peculiar kind,
For John's it buttoned up the front,
And Charlie's down behind.

Now these two brothers had a hat,
They bought it on a Monday,
And John wore it all the week,
But Charlie on the Sunday.

Now these two brothers kept a shop,
With buns and treacle-honey,
And John he sold the ginger pop
While Charlie took the money.

Now these two brothers had an ass,
And it was very thin,
John led it to the river bank,
And Charlie pushed it in.

Now these two brothers kept a cow,
'Twas also very thin
John filled it up with hydrogen,
Charles pricked it with a pin.

Now these two brothers had a boat,
And it was made of cork,
John helped to row it with a spoon
And Charlie with a fork.

There was a man who had two sons,
And these two sons were brothers,
And John it was the name of one,
And Charlie was the other's.

# The Quiet Old Man

Edward Lear

There was an Old Man who said, 'Hush!
I perceive a young bird in this bush!'
    When they said, 'Is it small?'
    He replied, 'Not at all!
It is four times as big as the bush!'

# *Be Kind to Animals*

## Anon

Speak gently to the herring and kindly to the calf,
Be blithesome with the bunny, at barnacles don't laugh!
Give nuts unto the monkey, and buns unto the bear,
Ne'er hint at currant jelly if you chance to see a hare!
Oh, little girls, pray hide your combs when tortoises draw
    nigh,
And never in the hearing of a pigeon whisper Pie!
But give the stranded jelly-fish a shove into the sea, –
Be always kind to animals wherever you may be!

Oh, make not game of sparrows, nor faces at the ram,
And ne'er allude to mint sauce when calling on a lamb.
Don't beard the thoughtful oyster, don't dare the cod to
    crimp,
Don't cheat the pike, or ever try to pot the playful shrimp.
Tread lightly on the turning worm, don't bruise the
    butterfly,
Don't ridicule the wry-neck, nor sneer at salmonfry;
Oh, ne'er delight to make dogs fight, nor bantams
    disagree, –
Be always kind to animals wherever you may be!

Be lenient with lobsters, and ever kind to crabs,
And be not disrespectful to cuttle-fish or dabs;
Chase not the Cochin-China, chaff not the ox obese,
And babble not of feather-beds in company with geese.
Be tender with the tadpole, and let the limpet thrive,
Be merciful to mussels, don't skin your eels alive;
When talking to a turtle don't mention calipee –
Be always kind to animals wherever you may be.

# Doctor Bell

Anon

Doctor Bell fell down the well
And broke his collar-bone.
Doctors should attend the sick
And leave the well alone.

# The Bearded Old Man

Edward Lear

There was an Old Man with a beard,
Who said, 'It is just as I feared!—
   Two Owls and a Hen,
   Four Larks and a Wren,
Have all built their nests in my beard!'

# The Young Lady of Ryde

Anon

There was a young lady of Ryde,
Who ate some green apples and died.
   The apples fermented
   Inside the lamented,
And made cider inside her inside.

# The Young Salesman of Leeds

Anon

There was a young salesman of Leeds,
Rashly swallowed six packets of seeds.
   In a month, silly ass,
   He was covered with grass,
And he couldn't sit down for the weeds.

# The Blind Men and the Elephant

## John Saxe

It was six men of Indostan,
　　To learning much inclined,
Who went to see the Elephant
　　(Though all of them were blind),
That each by observation
　　Might satisfy his mind.


The First approached the Elephant,
　　And, happening to fall
Against his broad and sturdy side,
　　At once began to bawl,
'God bless me! but the Elephant
　　Is very like a wall!'


The Second, feeling of the tusk,
　　Cried – 'Ho! what have we here
So very round and smooth, and sharp?
　　To me 'tis mighty clear
This wonder of an Elephant
　　Is very like a spear!'


The Third approached the animal
　　And happening to take
The squirming trunk within his hands,
　　Thus boldly up and spake:
'I see' – quoth he – 'the Elephant
　　Is very like a snake!'

The Fourth reached out his eager hand
    And felt about the knee:
'What most this wondrous beast is like
    Is mighty plain' – quoth he –
' 'Tis clear enough the Elephant
    Is very like a tree!'

The Fifth, who chanced to touch the ear,
    Said – 'E'en the blindest man
Can tell what this resembles most;
    Defy the fact who can,
This marvel of an Elephant
    Is very like a fan!'

The Sixth no sooner had begun
    About the beast to grope,
Than, seizing on the swinging tail
    That fell within his scope,
'I see' – quoth he – 'the Elephant
    Is very like a rope!'

And so these men of Indostan
    Disputed loud and long,
Each in his own opinion
    Exceeding stiff and strong,
Though each was partly in the right,
    And all were in the wrong!

# The Two Old Bachelors

## Edward Lear

Two old Bachelors were living in one house;
One caught a Muffin, the other caught a Mouse.
Said he who caught the Muffin to him who caught the
      Mouse, –
'This happens just in time, for we've nothing in the house,
Save a tiny slice of lemon and a teaspoonful of honey,
And what to do for dinner, – since we haven't any money?
And what can we expect if we haven't any dinner,
But to lose our teeth and eyelashes and keep on growing
      thinner?'

Said he who caught the Mouse to him who caught the
      Muffin, –
'We might cook this little Mouse if we only had some
      Stuffin'!
If we had but Sage and Onions we could do extremely
      well,
But how to get that Stuffin' it is difficult to tell!'

Those two old Bachelors ran quickly to the town
And asked for Sage and Onions as they wandered up and
      down;
They borrowed two large Onions, but no Sage was to be
      found
In the Shops or in the Market or in all the Gardens round.

But some one said, – 'A hill there is, a little to the north,
And to its purpledicular top a narrow way leads forth;

And there among the rugged rocks abides an ancient
    sage,—
An earnest Man, who reads all day a most perplexing
    page.
Climb up and seize him by the toes! – all studious as he
    sits,
And pull him down, and chop him into endless little bits!
Then mix him with your Onion (cut up likewise into
    scraps),
And your Stuffin' will be ready, and very good – perhaps.'

Those two old Bachelors, without loss of time,
The nearly purpledicular crags at once began to climb;
And at the top among the rocks, all seated in a nook,
They saw that Sage a-reading of a most enormous book.
'You earnest Sage!' aloud they cried, 'Your book you've
      read enough in! –
We wish to chop you into bits and mix you into Stuffin'!' –
But that old Sage looked calmly up, and with his awful
      book
At those two Bachelors' bald heads a certain aim he took; –
And over crag and precipice they rolled promiscuous
      down, –
At once they rolled, and never stopped in lane or field or
      town;
And when they reached their house, they found (besides
      their want of Stuffin')
The Mouse had fled; – and previously had eaten up the
      Muffin.

They left their home in silence by the once convivial door;
And from that hour those Bachelors were never heard of
      more.


## Paintwork

### Anon


A painter, who lived in Great Britain,
      Interrupted two girls with their knitain,
            He said, with a sigh,
            'That park bench – well I
      Just painted it, right where you're sitain.'

116

# The Old Man of Dumbree

## Edward Lear

There was an old man of Dumbree,
Who taught little owls to drink tea;
    For he said, 'To eat mice
    Is not proper or nice,'
That amiable man of Dumbree.

# The Wretched Man

## Anon

A wretched man walked up and down
To buy his dinner in the town.

At last he found a wretched place
And entered in with modest grace,

Took off his coat, took off his hat,
And wiped his feet upon the mat,

Took out his purse to count his pence
And found he had but two half-cents.

The bill of fare, he scanned it through
To see what two half-cents would do.

The only item of them all
For two half-cents was one fishball.

So the waiter he did call
And gently whispered: One fishball.

The waiter bellowed down the hall:
This gentleman here wants one fishball.

The diners looked both one and all
To see who wanted one fishball.

The wretched man, all ill at ease
Said: A little bread, sir, if you please.

The waiter bellowed down the hall:
We don't serve bread with one fishball.

The wretched man, he felt so small,
He quickly left the dining hall.

The wretched man, he went outside,
And shot himself until he died.

This is the moral of it all,
Don't ask for bread with one fishball.


## The Big Race

### Mrs Molesworth


A Daisy and a Buttercup
    Agreed to have a race,
A squirrel was to be the judge
    A mile off from the place.

The Squirrel waited patiently
    Until the day was done –
Perhaps he is there waiting still,
    You see – they couldn't run.

# Mr Daddy Long-Legs and Mr Floppy Fly

### Edward Lear

Once Mr Daddy Long-Legs,
  Dressed in brown and grey,
Walked about upon the sands
  Upon a summer's day;
And there among the pebbles,
  When the wind was rather cold,
He met with Mr Floppy Fly,
  All dressed in blue and gold.
And as it was too soon to dine,
They drank some Periwinkle-wine,
And played an hour or two, or more,
At battlecock and shuttledore.

Said Mr Daddy Long-Legs
  To Mr Floppy Fly,
'Why do you never come to court?
  'I wish you'd tell me why.
'All gold and shine, in dress so fine,
  'You'd quite delight the court.
'Why do you never go at all?
  'I really think you ought!
'And if you want, you'd see such sights!
'Such rugs! and jugs! and candle-lights!
'And more than all, the King and Queen,
'One in red, and one in green!'

'O Mr Daddy Long-Legs,'
  Said Mr Floppy Fly,
'It's true I never go to court,
  'And I will tell you why.
'If I had six long legs like yours,
   'At once I'd go to court!
'But Oh! I can't, because my legs
  'Are so extremely short.
'And I'm afraid the King and Queen
 '(One in red and one on green)
'Would say aloud, "You are not fit,
' "You Fly, to come to court a bit!"'

'O Mr Daddy Long-Legs,'
  Said Mr Floppy Fly,
 'I wish you'd sing one little song!
  'One mumbian melody!
'You used to sing so awful well
  'In former days gone by,
'But now you never sing at all;
  'I wish you'd tell my why:
'For if you would, the silvery sound
'Would please the shrimps and cockles round,
'And all the crabs would gladly come
'To hear you sing, "Ah, Hum di Hum!"'

Said Mr Daddy Long-Legs,
  'I can never sing again!
'And if you wish, I'll tell you why,
  'Although it gives me pain.
'For years I could not hum a bit,
  'Or sing the smallest song;

'And this the dreadful reason is,
    'My legs are grown too long!
'My six long legs, all here and there,
'Oppress my bosom with despair;
'And if I stand, or lie, or sit,
'I cannot sing one single bit!'

So Mr Daddy Long-Legs
    And Mr Floppy Fly
Sat down in silence by the sea,
    And gazed upon the sky.
They said, 'This is a dreadful thing!
    'The world has all gone wrong,
'Since one has legs too short by half,
    'The other much too long!
'One never more can go to court,
'Because his legs have grown too short;
'The other cannot sing a song,
'Because his legs have grown too long!'

Then Mr Daddy Long-Legs
    And Mr Floppy Fly
Rushed downward to the foaming sea
    With one sponge-taneous cry;
And there they found a little boat
    Whose sails were pink and grey;
And off they sailed among the waves
    Far, and far away.
They sailed across the silent main
And reached the great Grombolian plain;
And there they play for evermore
At battlecock and shuttledore.

# The Man in the Wilderness

## Anon

The man in the wilderness asked of me,
How many strawberries grow in the sea?
I answered him as I thought good,
As many red herrings as grow in the wood.

# Flight of Fancy

## Anon

There was an old man who averred
He had learned how to fly like a bird.
    Cheered by thousands of people
    He leapt from the steeple –
This tomb states the date it occurred.


# Epitaph for a Dentist

## Anon

Stranger! Approach this spot with gravity!
John Brown is filling his last cavity.


# At Peace with Peas

## Anon

I always eat peas with honey,
I've done it all my life,
They do taste kind of funny,
But it keeps them on the knife.

# Little Willie

## Anon

Willie, writing on the bed,
Spilt some ink on Mother's spread.
'Ma,' he said, when she came back,
'It will dye a lovely black!'

# The Optimist and the Pessimist

## Anon

'Twixt the optimist and the pessimist
   The difference is droll:
The optimist sees the doughnut
   While the pessimist sees the hole.

# Ooey-Gooey

## Anon

Ooey-Gooey was a worm.
    A mighty worm was he,
He sat upon the railroad track,
    A train he did not see;
Chuff chuff – splutter splutter
    Ooey-Gooey – Peanut Butter!


# A Deal of Faith

## Anon

There was a faith-healer of Deal,
Who said: 'Although pain isn't real,
    If I sit on a pin
    And it punctures my skin,
I dislike what I fancy I feel.'

# *Last Word*

## Robert Louis Stevenson

The world is so full of a number of things,
I'm sure we should all be as happy as kings.

# ILLUMINATED LIMERICKS

# CONTENTS

## INTRODUCTION

According to the dictionary, 'the five-line nonsense verse known as the Limerick originated with the eighteenth century ale-house chorus *Will you come up to Limerick?'*

Rubbish! McLachlan and I have been doing some serious research on the subject and we've unearthed loads of limericks that were doing the rounds way before the beginning of the eighteenth century. This one, for example, is more than five hundred years old:

> Ewe bleateth after lamb,
> Low'th after calve too.
> Bullock starteth
> Bucke farteth—
> Merry sing Cuckoo!

And look at this—without doubt the first limerick in the history of the world:

> In the Garden of Eden lay Adam
> Complacently stroking his madam,
> And loud was his mirth
> For on all of the earth
> There were only two balls—and he had 'em.

Of course that best-known limerick writer was that eminent Victorian Edward Lear (1812–1888):

> Although at the limericks of Lear
> We may be tempted to sneer
> We should never forget
> That we owe him a debt
> For his work as the first pioneer.

7

The trouble with Lear's limericks is that they do tend to be remarkably respectable . . .

> There was an old person from Twickenham
> Who whipped his four horses to quicken 'em;
> When they stood on one leg
> He said faintly 'I beg
> We may go back directly to Twickenham!'

. . . and the trouble with respectable limericks is that they do tend to be somewhat short on laughs . . .

> The Limerick packs laughs anatomical
> Into space that's quite economical.
> But the good ones I've seen
> So seldom are clean
> And the clean ones so seldom are comical.

Don't misunderstand us. We're honest, clean-living souls, like you. We don't want limericks that are coarse or crude. We are very well aware that a limerick has to be handled with care . . .

> The limerick is furtive and mean;
> You must keep it in close quarantine,
> Or it sneaks to the slums
> And promptly becomes
> Disorderly, drunk and obscene.

As far as we're concerned, in poetry—as in fancy dress —subtlety is all:

> There was a young woman from Acnos
> Who went to a party as Venus.
> We told her how rude
> 'Twas to go there quite nude,
> So we got her a leaf from the green-h'us.

In the course of our rigorous researches McLachlan and I have

8

come across limericks of every description—from limericks that celebrate the great intellectual giants of the age like this one:

There's a notable family named Stein:
There's Gertrude, there's Ep and there's Ein.
Gert's prose is the bunk
Ep's sculpture is junk
And no one can understand Ein!

—to limericks that don't look like limericks at all, like the advertisement once placed in the *Catholic Herald* by Monsignor Ronald Knox: 'Evangelical vicar in want of a portable secondhand font, would dispose of the same for a portrait (in frame) of the Bishop Elect of Vermont.'

But the limericks I have chosen and McLachlan has illuminated for this collection are the ones we feel suit the form best. We're both philosophers at heart, so in the pages that follow we've tried to create a unique A to Z of Life with Limericks. We're great believers in *joie de vivre*\* and by the time you've been through our book we hope you will be too.

R.K.

\*That's French for 'grin and bear it'.

# ANIMAL MAGIC.

An eccentric old person of Slough,
Who took all his meals with a cow,
Always said, 'It's uncanny,
She's so like Aunt Fanny,'
But he never would indicate how.

The village was giddy with rumours
Of a goat who was suffering from tumors,
Garbage, rubbish and waste
Were all to his taste—
But he choked on Elizabeth's bloomers.

There was an old lady of Herm,
Who tied bows on the tail of a worm;
Said she, 'You look festive,
But don't become restive,
You'll wriggle 'em off if you squirm.'

12

There was a young girl known as Sue
Who carried a frog in each shoe.
When asked to stop
She replied with a hop
'I'm trying to get in Who's Zoo!'

There was a young girl name of Clare
Who once was attacked by a bear.
While chased in a field
She tripped and revealed
Some meat to the bear that was rare.

13

Said a cat as he playfully threw
His wife down a well in Peru,
'Relax, dearest Thora,
Please don't be angora,
I was only artesian you.'

There was a young peasant named Gorse
Who fell madly in love with his horse.
Said his wife: 'You rapscallion
That horse is a stallion—
This constitutes grounds for divorce.'

There was a young maid from Madras
Who had a magnificent ass.
Not rounded and pink
As you probably think—
It was grey, had long ears, and ate grass.

Said an envious erudite ermine:
'There's one thing I cannot determine;
When a girl wears my coat
She's a person of note:
When I wear it I'm only called vermin.'

15

There once was a gnu in a zoo
Who tired of the same daily view.
To seek a new sight
He stole out one night,
And where he went gnobody gnu.

There was an Italian named Bruno
Who said: 'Loving is one thing I do know.
A woman is fine,
A man is divine,
But a sheep is Numero Uno.'

# BAD MANNERS.

I sat next to the Duchess at tea.
It was just as I feared it would be:
Her rumblings abdominal
Were simply phenominal,
And everyone thought it was me!

17

There once was a fellow called Sydney,
Who ate lots of pie—steak and kidney.
He ate so much crust
That they thought he would bust,
He ought to have known better—now didney?

It's the latest on-going thing I believe.

There was a young woman named Dotty
Who said as she sat on her potty,
'It isn't polite
To do this in sight,
But then who am I to be snotty?'

There was a young person from Tottenham
Whose manners, Good Lord! she'd forgotten 'em.
When she went to the Vicar's,
She took off her knickers,
Because she said she was hot in 'em.

We thought him an absolute lamb,
But when he sat down in some jam
On taking his seat
At our Sunday School treat,
We all heard the Vicar say: 'Damn!'

I don't mind if a girl rides a hel'copter,
I don't mind if a girl drives a car,
But the girl who rides straddle
An old fashioned saddle
Is stretching things just a bit far.

There was a young curate of Minster
Who admonished a giddy young spinster.
For she used, on the ice,
Words not at all nice
When he, at a turn, slid against her.

# CAMP FOLLOWERS.

There was a young man named Treet
Who minced as he walked down the street.
He wore shoes of bright red,
And playfully said,
'I may not be strong, but I'm sweet.'

A pansy who lived in Khartoum
Took a lesbian up to his room.
They argued all night
Over who had the right
To do what, and with which, and to whom.


There was a gay writer named Smith,
Whose virtue was largely a myth.
We knew that he did it;
He couldn't have hid it—
The question was only who with.

# DRESS SENSE.

A model called Suzy Dunbar
Committed a dreadful *faux pas;*
She loosened a stay
In her new *décolleté*
Exposing her *je ne sais quoi!*

There was a young lady of Wilts,
Who walked to the Highlands on stilts.
When they said, 'Oh, how shocking,
    To show so much stocking.'
She answered, 'Well, what about kilts?'

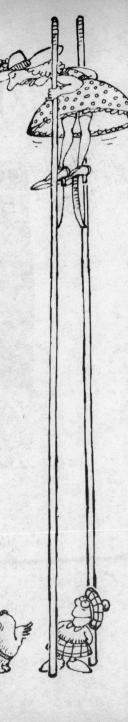

There was a fat lady of Clyde
Whose shoelaces once came untied;
She feared that to bend
Would display her rear end,
So she cried and she cried and she cried.

There once was a girl, Mabel Erskine,
Who had a remarkably fair skin.
When I said to her, 'Mabel,
You'd look well in sable.'
She answered, 'I'm best in my bearskin.'

25

There was a young lad of Penrose
Who had pockets in none of his clothe[s]
When asked by his lass
Where he carried his brass
He said: 'Darling, I pay through the no[se]'

There once was a lady called Harris
That nothing seemed apt to embarrass
Till the bubble-bath she poured
Into the tub she adored
Turned out to be plaster of Paris.

# EGOCENTRIC.

A self-centred old man called Keith
Sat down on his set of false teeth.
Said he, with a start,
'Oh Lor' bless my heart!
I have bitten myself underneath!'

I'd rather have fingers than toes;
I'd rather have ears than a nose;
And as for my hair,
I'm glad that it's there.
I'll be awfully sad when it goes.

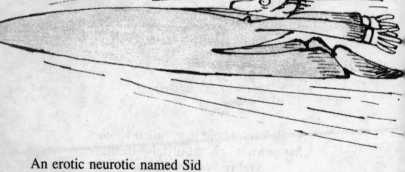

An erotic neurotic named Sid
Got his Ego confused with his Id,
His errant libido
Was like a torpedo,
And that's why he done what he did.

28

A young schizophrenic named Struther
When told of the death of his mother,
　　Said, 'Yes, it's too bad,
　　But I can't feel too sad.
After all, I *still* have each other.'


The girls who frequent pleasure palaces
Have no use for psychoanalysis.
　　And though Doctor Freud
　　Would be sorely annoyed,
They stick to their old-fashioned fallacies.

# FACTS OF LIFE.

Concerning the birds, bees and flowers
In the gardens, the fields and the bowers,
You will note at a glance
That their ways of romance
Are totally different from ours.

There was an old lady of Harrow
Whose views were exceedingly narrow.
At the end of her paths
She built two bird baths
For the different sexes of sparrow.

There was a young woman from Mulberry,
Whose knowledge of life was desultory,
She announced, like a sage,
'Adolescence is the stage
That comes between puberty and adultery.'

# GOLDEN OLDIES.

There was a young man of Devizes,
Whose ears were of different sizes.
The one that was small
Was of no use at all,
But the other won several prizes.

There was a faith-healer of Deal
Who said: 'Although pain isn't real,
If I sit on a pin,
And I punctures my skin,
I dislike what I fancy I feel.'

There was a young man of Bengal
Who went to a fancy-dress ball,
He went, just for fun,
Dressed up as a bun,
And a dog ate him up in the hall.

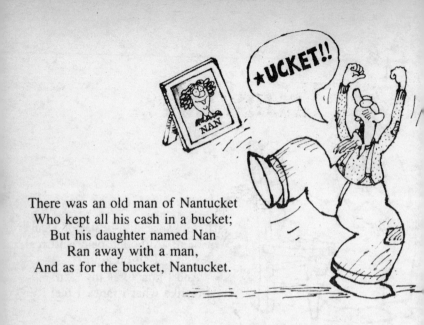

There was an old man of Nantucket
Who kept all his cash in a bucket;
But his daughter named Nan
Ran away with a man,
And as for the bucket, Nantucket.

Said a foolish householder from Wales
'A foul odour of gas prevails,'
She then struck a light—
And later that night
Was collected in seventeen pails.

34

# Holiday Snaps.

There was a young lady of Joppa
Who on holiday came quite a 'cropper;
  She went to Ostend
  With a gentleman friend—
But the rest of the tale is improper.

A signora who strolled down the Corso
Displayed quite a lot of her torso
A crowd soon collected
And no one objected,
Though some were in favour of more so.

A nudist resort at Benare
Took a midget in all unawa
But he made members we
For he just couldn't keep
His nose out of private affa

# Insulting Behaviour.

A girl who weighed many oz.
Used language I dare not pronoz.
For a fellow unkind
Pulled her chair out behind
Just to see (so he said) if she'd boz.

To an artist a husband named Thicket
Said: 'Turn your backside and I'll kick it.
You have painted my wife
In the nude to the life;
Do you think for one moment that's cricket?'

Said a vulgar old Earl, whom I knew:
'I've been struck from the rolls of Who's Who,
Just because I was found,
Lying prone on the ground
With the housemaid; and very nice too!'

There once was a maître d'hôtel
Who said, 'They can all go to hell!
They make love to my wife
And it ruins my life,
For the worst is, they do it so well!'

here was a strange creature named Marks
Whose idea of diversions and larks
Was stirring up tramps,
Disturbing scout log camps,
And defacing nude statues in parks.

A lady there was from Antigua,
Who remarked to her spouse 'What a pigua!'
He retorted 'My Queen,
Is it manners you mean?
Or do you refer to my figua?'

There was a young lady of Bude
Who walked down the street in the nude.
A policeman said, 'Whattum
Magnificent bottom!'
And slapped it as hard as he could.

# JUST A DROP.

There was a young fellow called Sydney,
Who drank till he ruined his kidney.
It shrivelled and shrank,
As he sat there and drank,
But he'd had a good time at it, didn' he?

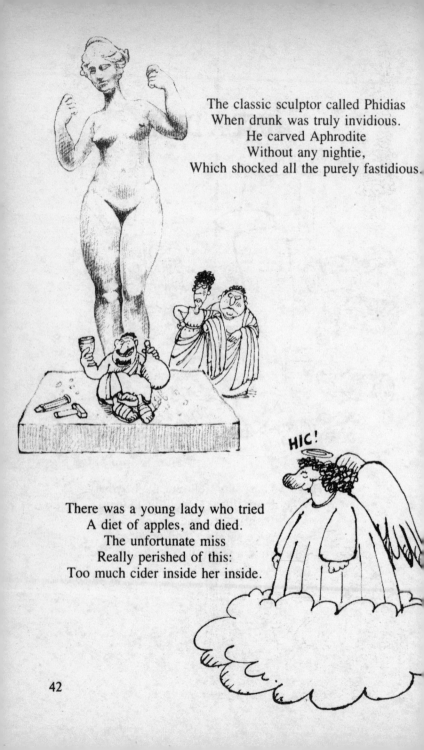

The classic sculptor called Phidias
When drunk was truly invidious.
He carved Aphrodite
Without any nightie,
Which shocked all the purely fastidious.

HIC!

There was a young lady who tried
A diet of apples, and died.
The unfortunate miss
Really perished of this:
Too much cider inside her inside.

42

There was a young girl whose frigidity
Approached cataleptic rigidity
Till you gave her a drink
When she quickly would sink
In a state of complaisant liquidity.

There was a young lady named Lynn
Who thought fornication a sin.
But when she was tight
It seemed quite all right—
So the fellows all filled her with gin.

14 men per gallon, dear

GIN

14 MPG

# KEEP FIT.

A lady, an expert on skis,
Went out with a man who said, 'Plis,
On the next precipice
Will you give me a kice?'
She said, 'Quick! Before somebody sis!'

When the tennis ball soared high above,
Nellie rose to receive it like a dove,
But the strain of her reach
Caused her knickers to breach
And her partner to cry out, 'That's love!'

There was a young lady of Venice,
Who used hard-boiled eggs to play tennis.
When they said, 'It seems wrong.'
She remarked, 'Go along!
You don't *know* how prolific my hen is!'

A young girl who was hopeless at tennis
And at swimming was really a menace
Took pains to explain:
'It depends how you train;
I was once a street-walker in Venice.'

There was a young maiden of Siam
Who said to her love, young Kiam,
'If you kiss me, of course
You will have to use force—
But God knows you are stronger than I am.'

# LITERARY LAPSES.

There was a young poet of Trinity

Who, although he could trill like a linnet, he

Could never complete

Any poem with feet,

Saying, 'Idiots,

Can't you see

that what I'm writing

happens

to be

Free

Verse?'

'For the tenth time, dull Daphnis,' said Chlo[
'You have told me my bosom is snowy;
You have made such verse on
Each part of my person
Now *do* something, there's a good boy!'

ODE TO
CHLOE'S
RIGHT
BRE

ODE TO
A TOAD

*you have lovely big* ......

Each time she sat down to complete her
Ode to the famous love cheater,
The things that he said
To get her to bed
Seemed to jump off the pages to metre.

48

If muses be the food of love....

There was a young poet of Thusis
Who took twilight walks with the Muses,
But these nymphs of the air
Are not quite what they were,
And the practice has led to abuses.

49

An authoress armed with a skew
Once hunted a hostile reviewe
'I'll teach you,' she cried,
As she punctured his hide,
'To call my last novel too pure

The late poet called Ogden Nash
Always made of his English a hash.
When asked where it led
He flippantly said,
'It gives it a great touch of clash.'

There's a clever old miser who tries
Every method to e-con-omize.
He said with a wink,
'I save gallons of ink
By simply not dotting my i's.'

# MUSICAL INTERLEWD.

There was an old bass of Boolong
Who frightened the birds with his song.
It wasn't the words
Which astonished the birds
But the horrible *dooble ontong*.

A young violinist from Rio
Was seducing a lady named Cleo.
As she took down her panties
She said, 'No andantes—
I want this *allegro con brio!*'

As Mozart composed a sonata
The maid bent to fasten her garter
Without delay
He started to play
*Un poco piu appasionata.*

# Nuptial Bliss.

The bride went up the aisle
In traditional virginal style,
But they say she was nary
An innocent cherry,
But a whore from the banks of the Nile.

A plumpish young lady from Eton
Whose delight was to read Mrs. Beeton
Said: 'Marry me, Jack,
And you'll find that my back
Is a nice place to warm your cold feet on.'

There once was a woman of Churston
Who thought her third husband the worst 'un,
For he justly was reckoned
Far worse than the second,
And her second was worse than the first 'un.

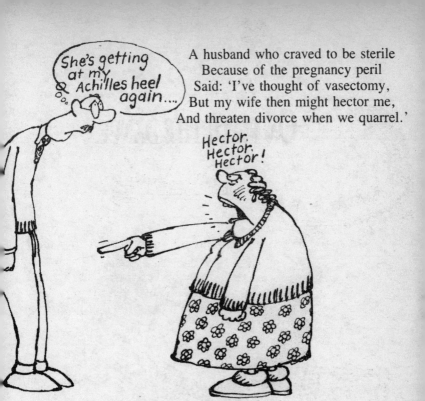

A husband who craved to be sterile
Because of the pregnancy peril
Said: 'I've thought of vasectomy,
But my wife then might hector me,
And threaten divorce when we quarrel.'

There was an old widower, Doyle,
Who wrapped up his wife in tin foil.
He thought it would please her
To stay in the freezer—
And, anyway, outside she'd spoil.

55

# ON WITH THE DANCE.

There was a young lady named Hall
Wore a newspaper dress to a ball.
The dress caught on fire
And burned her entire
Front page, sporting section and all.

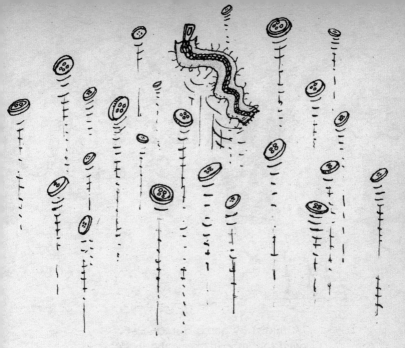

There was a young girl of Darjeeling
Who could dance with exquisite feeling
Not a murmur was heard,
Not a sound, not a word,
But the fly-buttons hitting the ceiling.


A strip-teaser on the Thames River
Caused a sensitive fellow to quiver.
The aesthetic vibration
Brought soulful elation.
Besides, it was good for his liver.


Three young girls from the Bahamas
Attended dance halls in pyjamas.
They were fondled all summer
By sax, bass, and drummer—
I'm surprised that they're not all now mamas.

57

A nudist by name Horace Sweet
Loved to dance in snow and in sleet,
    But one chilly December
    He froze every member,
And retired to a monkish retreat.

# PREGNANT PAUSES.

There was a young woman from Wantage
Of whom the Town Clerk took advantage.
Said the County Surveyor,
'Of course you must pay her;
You've altered the line of her frontage.'

There was a young lady from Thrace
Whose corsets no longer would lace.
    Her mother said, 'Nelly,
    There's more in your belly
Than ever went in through your face.'

There was a young lady of York
Who was shortly expecting the stork,
    When the doctor walked in
    With a businesslike grin,
A pick axe, a spade, and a fork.

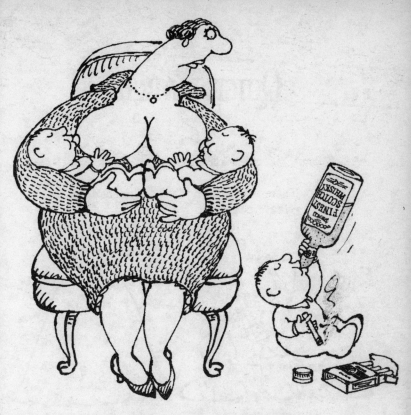

There was a young wife who begat
Three husky boys, Nat, Pat, and Tat.
They all yelled for food,
And a problem ensued
When she found there was no tit for Tat.


When twins came, their father Dann Dunn
Gave 'Edward' as name to each son.
When folks cried 'Absurd!'
He replied 'Ain't you heard
That two Eds are better than one?'

# QUICK MARCH!

There was a fierce soldier from Parma,
Who lovingly fondled his charmer.
　　Said the maiden demure,
　　'It's delightful, I'm sure,
But it's better without all that armour.'

There was a G.I. from Detroit
Who at kissing was very adroit;
   He could pucker his lips
     Into total eclipse,
Or open them out like a quoit.

The spouse of a pretty young thing
Came home from the wars in the spring.
   He was lame but he came
     With his dame like a flame—
A discharge is a wonderful thing.

# RELIGIOUS MANIA.

The Dean undressed with heaving breast
The Bishop's wife to lie on.
He thought it lewd
To do it nude
So he kept his old school tie on.

There was a young girl from Odessa,
A somewhat unblushing transgressor.
When sent to the priest
The lewd little beast
Began to undress her confessor.

There once was a monk in Siberia
Whose existence grew steadily drearier,
Till he broke from his cell
With one hell of a yell
And eloped with the Mother Superior.

A prelate of very high station
Was impeached by a pious relation.
He was found in a ditch
With—I won't say a witch—
But a woman of no education.

A potent young monk in a wood
Told a girl she should cling to the good
She obeyed him—and gladly!
He repulsed her—but sadly;
'My dear, you have misunderstood.'

66

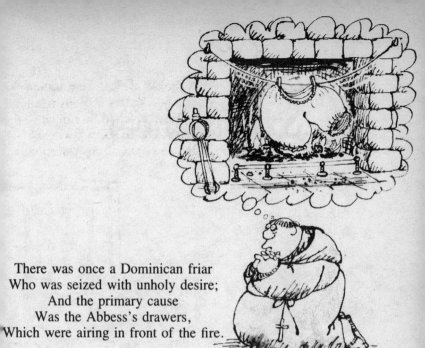

There was once a Dominican friar
Who was seized with unholy desire;
And the primary cause
Was the Abbess's drawers,
Which were airing in front of the fire.

There once was a monk of Gibraltar
Who wrote dirty jokes in his psalter.
An inhibited nun
Who had read every one
Made a vow to be laid on his altar.

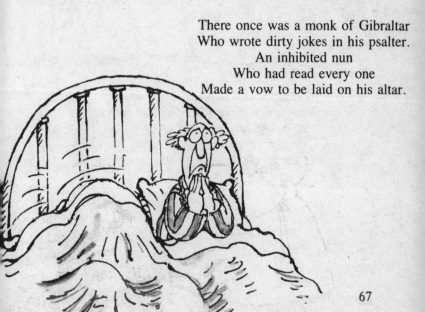

# Social Intercourse.

There was a young lady of Brent
Who said that she knew what it meant
When he asked her to dine,
Private room, lots of wine,
She knew, oh she knew!—but she went!

There was an old Duchess from Pitlochry
Whose morals were truly a mockery,
For under her bed
Was a lover instead
Of the usual porcelain crockery.

There is a young countess named Maude,
A frightful society fraud.
In company she
Is as cold as can be,
But get her alone—O my Gawd!

69

There is a young girl of Kilkenny
Who is worried by lovers so many
That the saucy young elf
Means to raffle herself,
And the tickets are two for a penny

There was a young lady of Leek
Who had fifty proposals a week.
Though she never grew tired
Of being admired,
She was often too sleepy to speak.

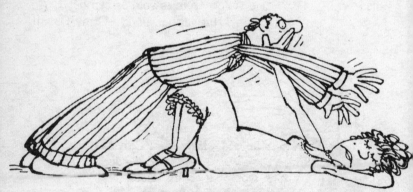

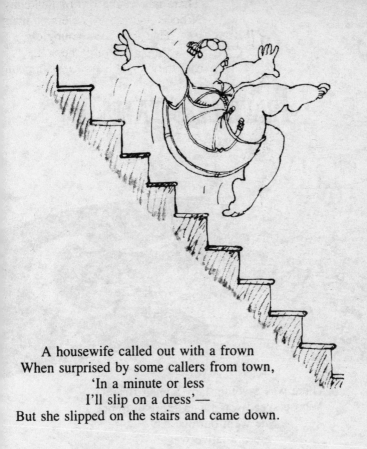

A housewife called out with a frown
When surprised by some callers from town,
   'In a minute or less
   I'll slip on a dress'—
But she slipped on the stairs and came down.


There was an old fellow from Croydon,
  Whose cook was a neat little hoyden.
    She would sit on his knees
    While shelling the peas
Or pleasanter duties employcd on.

# TRAVELLERS' TALES.

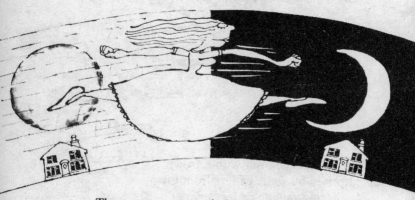

There was a young lady named Bright
Whose speed was far faster than light
She went out one day
In a relative way,
And returned the previous night.

There was a young lady of Spain
Who took down her pants on the train.
There was a young porter
Saw more than he orter,
And asked her to do it again.

A beautiful creature called Jane
Once kissed every man on a train;
Said she, 'Please don't panic;
I'm just nymphomanic—
It wouldn't be fun were I sane.'

There once was a fellow named Vane,
Whose leg was chopped off by a train.
When his friend said: 'How sad.'
He replied: 'It's not so bad,
For it's cured my varicose vein.'

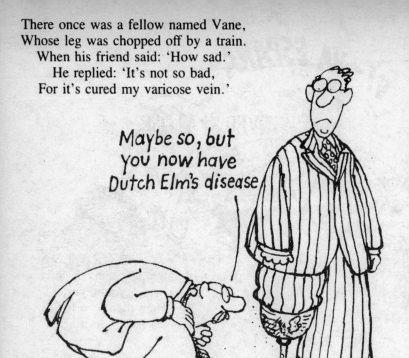

Maybe so, but
you now have
Dutch Elm's disease

There was a young fellow from Tyne
Put his head on the South-Eastern Line;
But he died of ennui,
For the 5.53
Didn't come till a quarter past nine.

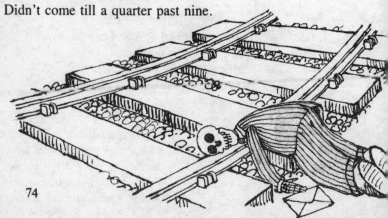

74

# UNLOVED & ALONE.

A homely old spinster of France
Who all men looked at askance,
Threw her skirt overhead
And then jumped into bed,
Saying, 'Now I've at least half a chance.'

A short-sighted spinster named White
Wore a suit of pyjamas one night.
As she happened to pass
In front of a glass
She exclaimed: 'There's a man!' in delight

There was once an old maid of Worcester
Who dreamt that a rooster seduced her.
She woke with a scream,
But 'twas only a dream—
A bump in the mattress had goosed her.

There was once a girl young and witty,
Who in looks was really quite pretty—
Yet one can't help but know
She has dreadful B.O.
As she's pretty and witty, it's a pity.

There was an old maid name of Rood,
Who was such an absolute prude
That she pulled down the blind
When changing her mind
Lest a libidinous eye should intrude.

# VULGAR TONGUES.

Incredible! Magnifique! Formidable!

There was a young girl of Tralee,
Whose knowledge of French was 'Oui, o
When they said: 'Parlez-vous?'
She replied: 'Same to you!'
And was famed for her bright repartee.

There was a young charmer named Sheba
Whose pet was a darling amoeba.
This queer blob of jelly
Would lie on her belly,
And blissfully murmur, 'Ich liebe.'


In Paris some visitors go
To see what no person should know
And then there are tourists,
The purest of purists,
Who say it is quite *comme il faut*.

There was a young fellow called Rex
With diminutive organs of sex.
When charged with exposure,
He said with composure:
*'De minimus no curat lex!'*

There was a young lady named Prentice
Who had an affair with a dentist.
To make the thing easier
He used anaesthesia,
And diddled her *non compos mentis*.

# WATER NYMPHS.

TRIPS AROUND THE BUXOM YOUNG LADY OF BUDE - £1

A buxom young lady of Bude
Remarked: 'Men are exceedingly rude;
When I bathe in the sea
They all follow me
To see if my bosoms protrude.

There was a young lady named Zanka
Who retired while the ship lay at anchor;
But awoke in dismay
When she heard the mate say:
'We must pull up the top sheet and spanker.'

There was a proud sailor named Bates
Who did the fandango on skates.
He fell on his cutlass
Which rendered him nutless
And practically useless on dates.

Once a bather's clothing was strewd
By winds that left her quite nude.
Soon a man came along—
And unless I am wrong
You expected this line to be lewd.


A fisherman off of Quobod
Said 'I'll catch that tuna, by God!'
But the high-minded fish
Resented his wish
And nimbly swam off with his rod.

# X-Censored.

In this book you will have to admit
There are certain rude words we omit.
It would be very bad luck
If you found the word f***
And we never, no never, use s***.

There were three young ladies of Birmingham
And this is the scandal concerning 'em.
As they knelt in their stalls
They tickled the *****
Of the Bishop engaged in confirming 'em.

# YOUTHFUL FANCIES.

A much-worried mother once said,
'My dear, you've been kissing young Fred
Since six; it's now ten.
Do it just once again,
And then think of going to bed.'

When her daughter got married in Bicester
Her mother remarked as she kissed her,
    'That fellow you've won
      Is sure to be fun—
Since tea he's kissed me and your sister.'

ere were once two young people of taste
Who were beautiful down to the waist
      So they limited love
        To the regions above,
And thus remained perfectly chaste.

A young girl who'd not be disgraced
Would flee from all lovers in haste.
It all went quite well
Till one day she fell . . .
She sometimes still dreams that she's chaste.

WELCOME BACK TO
MAIDENHEAD

A cautious young girl from Penzance
Decided to take just one chance.
She wavered, then lo,
She let herself go . . .
Now all of her sisters are aunts.

On Matilda's white bosom there leaned
    The cheek of an immature fiend,
      But she yanked up his head
      And sarcastically said,
'My boy! Won't you *ever* be weaned?'

    There was a young maid of Ostend,
    Who swore she's hold out to the end;
      But alas! half-way over,
      Twixt Calais and Dover,
    She done what she didn't intend.

# ZEST FOR LIFE.

A sculptor remarked, 'I'm afraid
I've fallen in love with my trade.
I'm much too elated
With what I've created
And, chiefly, the woman I've made.'

When Angelico worked in cerise,
For the angel he painted his niece.
In a heavenly trance
He pulled off her pants
And erected a fine altar-piece.

While Titian was mixing rose-madder
His model posed nude on a ladder.
Her position, to Titian,
Suggested coition,
So he climbed up the ladder and had 'er.

A greedy young lady named Dee,
Went to bed with each man she did see.
When it came to the test
She wished to be best,
And practice makes perfect, you see.

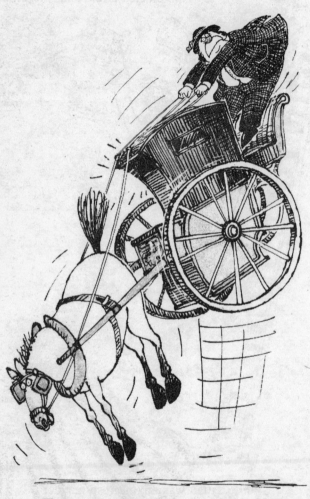

There was a young lady named Ransom
Who was indulged in three times in a hansom.
When she cried out for more
A voice from the floor
Said, 'My name is Simpson, not Samson.'

There was a young lady of Exeter,
So pretty, that men craned their necks at her.
One was even so brave
As to take out and wave
The distinguishing mark of his sex to her.

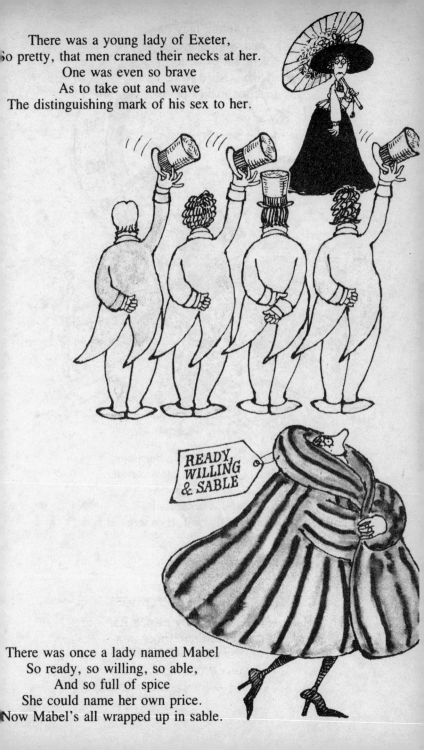

READY,
WILLING
& SABLE

There was once a lady named Mabel
So ready, so willing, so able,
And so full of spice
She could name her own price.
Now Mabel's all wrapped up in sable.

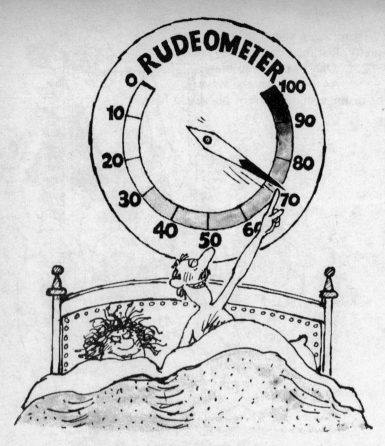

I wooed a stewed nude in Bermuda,
I was rude, but by God! she was ruder.
She said it was crude—
To be wooed in the nude—
I pursued her, subdued her, then screwed her!


'Austerity now is the fashion,'
Remarked a young lady with passion.
Then she glanced at the bed,
And quietly said,
'But there's one thing no one can ration.'

There was a young lady of Norway
Who hung by her heels from a doorway.
She said to her boy
'Just look at me, Roy,
I think I've discovered one more way.'


Said a beautiful girl named Elaine,
'I like it just now and again;
But I wish to explain
That by, 'Now and again'
I mean now and *again* and AGAIN.

God's plan made a hopeful beginning,
But man spoiled his chances by sinning.
We trust that God's Glory
Will end up the story,
But at present the other side's winning!